NORTHWEST WINE

The Premium Grape Wines of Oregon, Washington, and Idaho

Second Edition, Revised

by Ted Meredith

maps by Cynthia Lenz

Nexus Press
Kirkland, Washington

Library of Congress Catalog Card Number: 83-61863

ISBN 0-936666-02-1

Additional copies may be obtained by sending $8.95 (Washington residents also include sales tax) plus 95¢ for shipping to:

Nexus Press
P.O. Box 437
Kirkland, WA 98033.

Bookseller rates available on request.

Printed in the United States of America by
Snohomish Publishing, Snohomish, Washington.

CONTENTS

WASHINGTON

PREFACE

Perhaps a few words about the intent of this book are in order. The Northwest is an exceptional wine producing region in many ways. The Northwest's grape wine industry is based entirely on the *Vitis vinifera* grape species, the species responsible for all the world's greatest wines. The famous French Bordeaux and Burgundy wines are made from vinifera grapes. Cabernet Sauvignon, Chardonnay, Pinot Noir, and Riesling are examples of vinifera varieties. Except for California, the Northwest is the only major American winegrowing region based on premium vinifera grape wines. Most other regions rely heavily on native American species or French-American hybrids. Premium grape wines are the glory of the Northwest region. Fruit and berry wines are good in their own way, but they are different. This book is about the premium grape wines of Oregon, Washington, and Idaho—a distinctive art form very special to the Northwest.

A few very small wineries make wine from grape juice imported from outside the Northwest region. These wineries are given only brief mention, or none at all. The few fruit and berry wineries in this book are included only because they have demonstrated an understanding of premium grape wines and produce them in significant quantities. This book includes only wineries that are in operation and producing wine as of this writing. Many new wineries are about to begin production or are in their formative stages. Reportage of these wineries as they "come on stream" is left to the periodicals.

This book is not written only for regional consumption. Perhaps to the disappointment of some, every other sentence is not inflated with chauvinistic adjectives. In the production of premium grape wines in America, the Northwest is quantitatively second only to California, and, if the author may here be permitted a brief, unabashed, chauvinistic digression, the Northwest is qualitatively second to none. This does not mean that every Northwest wine meets the region's own high standard. Northwest grape growing and winemaking is unique. Much has been learned in just the past few years, and some grape growers and winemakers learn faster than others. The Northwest is easily one of America's most important winegrowing regions. It deserves not only regional chauvinistic enthusiasm, but the well-considered attention of the nation's wine drinkers. Part of the purpose of this book is to serve, at least in some small way, this end.

For those who are able to partake in the additional pleasure of visiting the wineries themselves, a few other points are in order. Wineries sometimes change visiting hours, and occasionally, even change locations. If the success of a trip to Northwest wine country is dependent on visiting a particular winery, calling or writing ahead is advised. In most instances, maps for urban wineries are not included in this book. A standard city map is the most effective tool for finding one's way to wineries in the major cities.

A final point, and an important one, Washington wine does not taste like Oregon wine does not taste like Idaho wine does not taste like California wine does not taste like French Burgundy does not taste like French Bordeaux does not taste like Italian Barolo does not taste like Spanish Rioja . . .

While the comparison of wines is part of their enjoyment, each wine deserves to be judged on its own merit. All too often, in our quest for objectivity and the security that it promises us, an arbitrary standard of taste is imposed, and wines are judged on their conformance with this "standard." Fine wines deserve better, and so do we. It is the differences, after all, the complex interplay of flavors and scents that drew us to premium wines in the first place. Fine wine, above all, is to be enjoyed.

Ted Meredith
Kirkland, Washington
July, 1983

NORTHWEST WINE

THE NORTHWEST REGION

For a time, Oregon and Washington wines had been grouped together under the nominal heading "wines of the Pacific Northwest," but Idaho has become very much a part of the region's wine industry, and in many ways, the Pacific Northwest appellation has always been a bit misleading. The name implies that all the major growing areas are under the influence of a marine climate, yet only in Oregon is this so. The appellation "Northwest wine" more genuinely reflects the nature of the region.

The Northwest region is by no means a unified growing climate, nor is it even a general macroclimate comprised of a number of microclimates. The region consists of two major, and very different, growing climates as well as innumerable smaller climates within the two major distinctions. The Cascade Mountain Range, running north to south through Washington and Oregon, divides these two climates. West of the Cascades, the climate is moderated by marine air from the Pacific Ocean. East of the Cascades, the climate is much warmer, drier, and sunnier. Because of other factors affecting the climate, nearly all of Washington's grapes are grown east of the Cascade Mountain Range, while nearly all of Oregon's grapes are grown west of the Cascades.

Regardless of growing area, the Northwest grape wine industry is based entirely on *Vitis vinifera*, the grape species responsible for all of the premium wine grapes, including Cabernet Sauvignon, Pinot Noir, Chardonnay, and Riesling. Except for California, no other major American winegrowing area can make such a claim. Although occasional examples exist of wines made from hybrid and native American grapes, one would be hard pressed to find any for sale.

It is important to remember that, although the growing climates in the Northwest region have similarities, the differences are many and quite dramatic. Since, for example, Washington and Oregon are adjacent states, it would be easy to assume that the wines from their major growing areas would be quite similar. Such is not the case. The wines are, for the most part, as radically different as their growing climates. Both are good. Both have proponents for their respective styles. And both deserve to be judged and enjoyed on their own merit. The chapters for each state outline the differences in more detail, but it is well to keep in mind that the Northwest region is a general geographic designation. In no way does it imply a single growing climate or a single style of wine.

THE WINE INDUSTRY

The rise in the Northwest wine industry has been meteoric. In 1963, the Northwest had one commercial vinifera winery. By 1983, there were well over fifty. In just the last five years, the number of premium grape wineries has more than doubled.

For many years, the wines of the Northwest were little known outside the region. Production was modest, and all the wine could be sold without resorting to outside markets. Sales to other states were primarily for the purposes of "spreading the word," or in a few cases, for establishing a marketing base for future production, a future that is now here.

Dramatic production increases in the Northwest wine industry are coming just at the time when the American wine industry as a whole is experiencing a slump. Consumer demand, while still increasing, is progressing at a slower rate, and, at the same time, the stronger U.S. dollar is inviting competition from foreign wines. For larger Northwest wineries, markets outside the region are an immediate necessity, and many smaller wineries are now feeling the need for sales in other states.

For years, the wine industry has not had to cope with the difficulties of a national marketing campaign. For those within the region it is difficult to comprehend that, to wine drinkers in other states, Northwest wines are not a routinely sought after purchase as are other wines such as Bordeaux or California Chardonnay. To the American consumer, Northwest wines are virtually unknown, wines to be purchased only occasionally out of curiosity or to "try something different." For years, modest production has limited availability, and correspondingly, lack of availability has meant lack of widespread interest. The industry is now achieving a production that will insure broad distribution. Interest and recognition will follow, though there will inevitably be a lag. The length of the lag is crucial to the health of the Northwest wine industry.

The transition will not be slow and steady. The need is immediate, and those within the wine industry are rallying to the

9

challenge. Washington has formed the Washington Wine Institute, patterned after California's own highly successful organization, and the once loosely associated Oregon Winegrowers Association has engaged the services of a public relations firm. The next several years may not be easy, but the payoff will come when the long underrecognized Northwest wine industry finally receives the attention and acclaim it deserves.

The sixties and seventies marked the birth of the Northwest wine industry, the early years of searching and experimentation gradually giving way, in vintage after vintage, to a thematic understanding of the growing climate, what it has to offer, and what it expects of the winegrower to bring out its best. This thematic interaction is, of course, an unending process, but the Northwest wine industry is now firmly established. The meteoric growth period that began in the late seventies sets the stage for the decade of the eighties.

CLIMATE MEASUREMENT

In evaluating a new winegrowing area, it is often helpful to compare its winegrowing climate with the climates of Europe. Yet in an anxious effort to validate an area, comparisons are sometimes made that are more misleading than revealing. It is always tempting for those in a new wine region to emphasize its similarities with famous, well-established regions, and at the same time, largely ignore any differences in an attempt to achieve immediate recognition and credibility. These temptations must be resisted, however, in the interests of a deeper understanding of the true merits of a new winegrowing region. Although the chapters on the individual states and wineries should provide a thematic basis for understanding Northwest growing climates, the following outlines a few of the factors pertaining to their evaluation.

The American wine industry's primary analytical tool for evaluating winegrowing climates is the heat summation method formulated at the University of California at Davis. When comparisons are drawn between a new winegrowing region and European growing climates, heat unit measurements inevitably become part of the discussion. Comparative climatic evaluation is obtained by totaling the number of degrees the average daily temperature is above

50 degrees for all the days of the growing season. If, for example, the average daily temperature is 65 degrees, 15 heat units (65-50 = 15) would be added to the year's total. The mean of the day's high and low temperatures is generally considered the average daily temperature. The yearly totals are divided into five summation ranges or "regions" for climate comparison.

Though perhaps the single most useful measurement of a growing climate, heat summation is a much rougher guide than popularly presumed, and especially outside of California, particularly in the Northwest, its limitations are increasingly apparent. Each of the five heat summation regions has a broad range, lumping together in the cooler regions climatic differences that are critical to the performance of premium grape varieties. A daily high and low of 72 degrees and 68 degrees has the same heat unit value as a daily high and low of 100 degrees and 40 degrees, yet such temperatures during grape ripening would have considerably different implications, as would a daily high of 90 degrees maintained for one hour versus a 90 degree high maintained for 10 hours.

The similarity of heat units is admittedly one of the most important keys in determining if a region can produce premium wines, yet many regions in America have heat units similar to those of European growing climates, but are completely unsuitable for grape growing. Among other basic climatic requirements is the necessity for winters cool enough to allow the vines to become dormant, but not cold enough to kill them, and the necessity for a growing season long enough to ripen the grapes. Beyond the basic factors, countless variables come into play. Day length (latitude), duration and range of maximum and minimum temperatures, nighttime cooling, cloud cover, soil reflectance, and heat during grape ripening versus heat during the vegetative period are a few of the many considerations contributing to the character of the grape, and ultimately, the quality of the wine.

Heat unit measurements as quality indicators are most useful and reliable when these other factors are held relatively constant, which is to say, within a narrowly delimited climatic and geographic region. Clearly, however, the world's winegrowing climates and geography vary widely, and these other factors are always in play. European viticulture is generally more attentive to these factors, but the wine industry is far from any comprehensive system of analysis, and particularly in the Northwest, where growing conditions vary significantly, these other factors define key viticultural differences—and remain largely unmeasured.

OREGON

Oregon Wineries

1. Adelsheim Vineyard
2. Alpine Vineyards
3. Amity Vineyards
4. Arterberry, Ltd.
5. Bjelland Vineyards
6. Chateau Benoit Winery
7. Cote des Colombes Vineyard
8. Elk Cove Vineyards
9. Ellendale Vineyards
10. The Eyrie Vineyards
11. Forgeron Vineyard
12. Glen Creek Winery
13. Henry Winery
14. Hidden Springs Winery
15. Hillcrest Vineyard
16. Hinman Vineyards
17. Hood River Vineyards
18. Knudsen Erath Winery
19. Mulhausen Vineyards
20. Oak Knoll Winery
21. Ponzi Vineyards
22. Serendipity Cellars Winery
23. Shafer Vineyard Cellars
24. Siskiyou Vineyards
25. Sokol Blosser Winery
26. Tualatin Vineyards
27. Valley View Vineyard
28. Wasson Brothers Winery

14

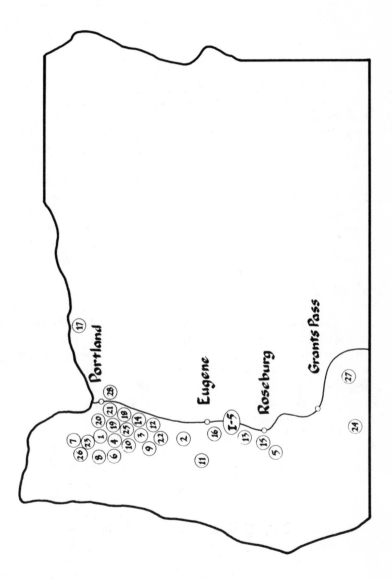

THE WINE INDUSTRY

On average, Oregon's wineries are much smaller than those of either Washington or Idaho. The Oregon industry is not dominated by huge vineyards or large agricultural corporations, nor has there been a lengthy heritage of post-prohibition winegrowing from which larger wineries might have evolved. Knudsen Erath, Sokol Blosser, and Tualatin are Oregon's largest, though none produce more than 100,000 gallons a year.

Oregon winegrowers are frequently white collar professionals who have turned to winegrowing in pursuit of their interest in fine wines, or who view winegrowing as a natural outlet for their desire for a rural lifestyle. Oregon has virtually no urban wineries. Nearly all are winery estates. The winery and winegrower's residence are adjacent to the vineyards, and the winegrower literally lives with his vines and wines. In most instances, winegrowing is chosen not because it is the easiest way to make money (which in Oregon, it surely is not), but out of an abiding commitment to the enterprise itself and the profound belief that Oregon winegrowers are pioneers in the most qualitatively important winegrowing region in America.

Winegrowers first coming to Oregon brought with them viticultural and winemaking practices learned from U.C. Davis, practices that worked well in California, but were not always well suited to Oregon's cooler climate. Many Oregon winegrowers are now turning to European sources, not simply to adopt "Old World" practices, but to take advantage of extensive technical research relating to winegrowing in cooler climates.

The Oregon trend toward closer vine spacing is one example of the European influence. Many early growers spaced their vines six to eight feet apart in rows with ten to twelve feet between each row. It is now believed that, in Oregon, closer spacing contributes to better ripening and varietal intensity, and more reliable crop yields. The Knudsen Erath winery has interplanted some of their original vineyards, and Elk Cove, a newer winery, has planted their vineyard at a six foot by seven foot spacing, a vine density of 1,054 plants per acre.

Although vinifera wines were made in Oregon in the late 1800's, Oregon's modern vinifera wine industry began just over twenty years ago when Richard Sommer came to the Umpqua Valley near Roseburg, planted wine grapes, and bonded Hillcrest

Vineyard two years later in 1963. Sommer focused his efforts on Riesling, and today, the grape remains a mainstay of Oregon's wine industry.

In 1965, two years after Hillcrest was bonded, David Lett came to Oregon with the singular intent of finding a climate suitable for the Burgundian grape varieties, and most particularly, a climate for Pinot Noir. Passing by the warmer Roseburg area in southern Oregon, Lett settled in the Dundee Hills in the Willamette Valley near Portland and founded The Eyrie Vineyards.

Pinot Noir is Oregon's stellar wine grape. Because of the white wine boom, most Northwest grape growers are planting very few red wine grapes. Oregon Pinot Noir is the exception, though Oregon, too, is caught up in the white wine frenzy.

The potential for Pinot Noir was apparent from the earliest years, but the Oregon wine industry as a whole was late in fully coming to terms with the grape. This widespread renaissance did not occur until roughly 1979, a vintage in which favorable growing conditions coincided with the maturation of many vineyards, the coming on stream of many new wineries, and better and more widespread understanding of viticultural and winemaking practices as they pertain to the Oregon climate. Visiting the wineries during the late 70's and early 80's was an exciting time. It was apparent that some of the best wines were still in the barrel, and that it would only be a relatively short time before Oregon would become famous for its Pinot Noir.

One of the 1960's pioneers, Dick Erath, in partnership with Cal Knudsen, was among the first to produce Pinot Noirs of distinction. Following the Erath and Eyrie wines through the 1970's offered a thematic look at the nature of Oregon Pinot Noir, vintage variations and characteristics, and a first glimpse at the range of stylistic interpretations available to Oregon winegrowers, a stylistic range not only extended and broadened in later years by these two wineries themselves, but by the many new wineries that have followed.

It might seem to some that Oregon Pinot Noir is accorded undue attention at the expense of the state's other vinous accomplishments, but if it is news when a new region produces fine wine, it is doubly so if that wine happens to be Pinot Noir, an exceptionally good grape that rarely does well outside of Burgundy.

Paradoxically, for this relatively cool American winegrowing climate, some Oregon wines, particularly Pinot Noir and Chardonnay, may seem a bit low in acid for those accustomed to their European counterparts. It is almost as if many Oregon winemakers unconsciously feel the need to release wines with lower acid levels to suit what has been variously termed the American/California/West Coast palate. Oregon Pinot Noir, in particular, suffers from this tendency. The wine typically has ample fruit, body, and suppleness to carry higher acid levels well. As the industry and popular palate mature, there will undoubtedly be a trend toward releasing Oregon wines with acid levels more befitting their viticultural heritage.

Pinot Noir, Riesling, and Chardonnay are Oregon's "big three" wine grapes. Most wineries produce some of each. Riesling is important, not only because it grows well, but also because it has wide popular appeal and can be released soon after the vintage, providing much needed cash flow for Oregon's new wineries. Chardonnay is another mainstay. Although it requires much attention in the vineyard, and challenges the skills of the winemaker, it is at the same time a flexible grape, adapting to a wide range of styles and growing climates. Premium sparkling wine may play a significant role in Oregon's future. Pinot Noir and Chardonnay, the classic Champagne grapes, both grow well in Oregon and ripen at lower sugar levels, an important criterion for premium sparkling wine.

The economics of Oregon winegrowing are hard. Vines are cane pruned rather than cordon pruned, a method requiring greater skill, attention, and time. Crop yields are small. Some years are too cool. Rain during harvest is not uncommon, and each year's crop faces destruction by unending waves of migrating robins. Oregon is not the easiest region in America to produce fine wine, but it is one of the best.

WINEGROWING CLIMATES

Virtually the entire Oregon winegrowing industry is located in the western part of the state in a long strip of land bordered on the west by the Coast Range and on the east by the foothills of the Cascade Range. Both mountain ranges run the entire north to south length of Oregon, and delimit and define the state's winegrowing region. The Coast Range, less mountainous than the Cascade Range, is enough of a climatological barrier that it partially blocks the wet, cool, marine air from the coast, yet still allows the moderating marine influence to temper the winegrowing climate. Frost and winter freezing are rarely problems, but for the northern half of the state, rain during harvest can be a problem. The climate is temperate. Grape ripening does not come with a rush, but gradually, as summer changes into fall.

It is a fundamental tenet of Oregon winegrowers that the best wines are made when the ripening of the grapes coincides with the ending of the growing season. A growing climate that ripens the grapes rapidly, early, and easily is also a climate that robs the grapes of complexity and nuance. In Europe's best growing regions, vintages vary considerably from year to year, and in these cool marginal climates, the vintages that are less good are almost always so because the year was too cool, rarely because the year was too warm or the grapes overripened or ripened too soon. Grape varieties are not grown where they will ripen easily, but where they will only just ripen in most years— and no more. In the best growing regions, it is expected that in some years the grapes will not fully ripen, a necessary paying of dues for the excellence of other years. It is not merely out of tradition, for example, that Pinot Noir is not grown in Bordeaux, where it would consistently produce "big" wines and ripen easily every year. Because Pinot Noir ripens more quickly than the Bordeaux varieties, it requires a cooler climate, and is thus grown in the cooler Burgundy region. It is these perspectives and this philosophy of winegrowing that has drawn Oregon winegrowers to the region and motivated and sustained them through the difficult pioneering years of the 60's and early 70's.

The northern Willamette Valley is Oregon's winegrowing heartland. Nearly all the vineyards are west of the river on the slopes of innumerable drainages that form the valley's many microclimates. At the northernmost end of the valley are Cote des Colombes, Elk Cove, Oak Knoll, Ponzi, Shafer, Tualatin, and Wasson Brothers. Outside the valley proper, in the Columbia River Gorge to the east, is Hood River Vineyards. Further south in the Willamette Valley near Newberg, McMinnville, and Salem are Adelsheim, Amity, Arterberry, Chateau Benoit, Ellendale, Eyrie, Glen Creek, Hidden Springs, Knudsen Erath, Mulhausen, Serendipity, and Sokol Blosser.

At Eugene, half way down the state, the broad Willamette Valley draws to a close as the foothills of the Coast Range and Cascades converge. Eugene itself has a climate very similar to the northern Willamette, but certain nearby slopes are significantly warmer and drier. Pinot Noir is still by far the predominant red wine grape, but Cabernet Sauvignon, in small quantities, is more in evidence than in the northern Willamette. Hinman, Alpine, and Forgeron are located in separate and distinct microclimates to the west and northwest of Eugene.

Further south near Roseburg, two thirds down the state, in an area that is warmer still, Bjelland, Henry, and Hillcrest are nestled in the drainages of the Umpqua River. The grape varieties grown in this area are as much dependent on the microclimates and individual preferences of the wineries as they are on the overall climate. Riesling, Chardonnay, Pinot Noir, and Cabernet Sauvignon all do well.

In the Applegate and Illinois Valleys near the California border are the Valley View and Siskiyou wineries. The Applegate Valley is the warmest and driest growing climate in Oregon. The Illinois Valley ranks a close second. Chardonnay does well in this environment, though its character is, not unexpectedly, markedly different from the Chardonnays of the northern Willamette. Except for certain cooler microclimates, Cabernet Sauvignon is the red wine grape of choice.

GRAPE VARIETIES

The following is not an exhaustive list of all the grape varieties grown in Oregon, but a review of those varieties that are grown in significant quantity, hold unusual promise, or are otherwise of special interest.

CABERNET SAUVIGNON, not a major grape for most of Oregon, does best in the southern part of the state. Some excellent Cabernets have been produced in the northern two thirds of Oregon in the Umpqua and Willamette valleys, but little is planted, and it does well only in the best sites in the warmest vintages. In the Illinois and Applegate valleys near the California border, however, Cabernet is the predominant red varietal, and shows excellent promise.

CHARDONNAY is Oregon's premier white wine grape. Along with Pinot Noir and Riesling, it is one of Oregon's most widely planted varieties. Of the three principal varieties, it is the most fickle, presenting problems for grower and winemaker alike. Though winemaking styles differ, Oregon Chardonnay typically goes through a major malolactic fermentation that dramatically drops its acidity, softens and rounds the wine, and transforms the fruit of the grape into other flavors. The majority of Oregon Chardonnays have no clear style referent in either California or Burgundy, but a distinctive style of their own, moderately full-bodied, yet delicate, and, depending on the winemaker, soft with moderate acidity, almost to a fault.

GEWURZTRAMINER, produced in small quantities by many Oregon wineries, successfully avoids the classic faults of the grape when it is grown outside its Alsatian homeland. Its sometimes heavy, flat, bitter, or "juicy fruit" attributes are minimized or eliminated, and though Oregon Gewurztraminers are not usually exceptionally distinguished, they are quite good, and find favor with those who enjoy this distinctive grape.

MERLOT, in Oregon, makes very fine wine. Unfortunately, it makes very few grapes. Unless conditions are just right, Merlot refuses to set berries, and in Oregon, during berry-set, conditions are seldom just right. Growers have experienced successive years with no crop at all. Needless to say, very little acreage is devoted to the grape. Growers in southern Oregon experience the problem to a much lesser degree, and Merlot may become a significant grape in that part of the state, perhaps with the aid of refined clonal selection.

MULLER-THURGAU, once purported to be a cross of Riesling and Sylvaner, yields high quantities of soft, pleasant, Riesling-like wine. The grape is naturally low in acid and does best in cooler growing sites. Muller-Thurgau is not widely planted, though a few wineries are emphasizing it as a speciality item.

PINOT GRIS, a genetic relative of Pinot Noir, may someday become one of Oregon's most important white wine grapes. As yet, the grape is planted only in miniscule quantities. At its worst, Pinot Gris can be heavy, flat, and dull, but given the right growing climate, and Oregon's Willamette Valley is such a climate, Pinot Gris can be a crisp, full-bodied, full-flavored wine of distinction.

In Oregon, Pinot Gris ripens well and produces reliably. Commercially, without a well-known name like Chardonnay or Riesling, Pinot Gris has much to overcome, but the strength of Oregon's wine industry is its unique capacity for producing wines that few other growing regions can produce successfully. Pinot Gris may join its cousin Pinot Noir as one of Oregon's special grape varieties.

21

PINOT NOIR, without question, is Oregon's stellar wine grape. Produced in all of Oregon's growing regions, it is the special star of the Willamette Valley where it dominates the wine scene. One of the world's noble grape varieties, Pinot Noir rarely does well outside of its French homeland in Burgundy, making Oregon's success with this difficult but rewarding grape all the more remarkable.

This is not to say that Oregon Pinot Noir tastes just like French Burgundy. Burgundies themselves range widely in style and flavor, and though the styles of Oregon Pinot Noir and French Burgundy intersect, Oregon Pinot Noir, especially when young, typically displays more forward spicy fruit, but less of the pleasant earthy dankness characteristic of many Burgundies.

French Burgundy is usually much higher in acid than most Oregon Pinot Noir. Regrettably, many Oregon winemakers choose to release Pinot Noir with relatively modest acidity, perhaps to appease what they view as the popular palate. Wines with higher acidity better complement food, are capable of longer cellaring, and do better justice to the grape.

Recent Pinot Noirs are consistently better than those of just a few years ago. Winegrowers are learning more how to make the wine, and the vines themselves are getting older and producing better quality fruit. Further improvement is ahead for this already excellent wine.

RIESLING, also known as White Riesling and Johannisberg Riesling, is the foundation of the Oregon wine industry, the first varietal planted in any quantity, and the wine that beginning wine drinkers most readily enjoy. Usually made in a semi-sweet style, Oregon Riesling is flavorful, crisp, and piquant. Often bottled, sold, and consumed within a year of the harvest, Riesling provides new wineries with quick cash flow and consumers with a pleasant drink. In better years, however, the wine needs and deserves a little cellar aging to bring out its best.

SAUVIGNON BLANC, also called Fume Blanc, is grown in small quantities from the California border to the northern Willamette Valley. The Willamette produces very fine Sauvignon Blanc in some vintages, but the climate is marginal for this varietal. Southern Oregon offers a more reliable climate for the grape, and production there should increase in future years.

SEMILLON, a genetic relative of Sauvignon Blanc, displays many of that grapes same grassy-herbaceous flavors. Semillon does well in southern Oregon, and acreage, though small, is increasing.

OREGON WINERIES

GROWN, PRODUCED & BOTTLED BY ADELSHEIM VINEYARD
NEWBERG, OREGON, USA, BW-OR-71, ALCOHOL 12½% BY VOL.

Adelsheim Vineyard
Founded 1978
Route 1, Box 129-D, Newberg, Oregon 97132
(503) 538-3652

Adelsheim Vineyard is not open to the public except for periodic special events. Those wishing to attend should write to Adelsheim for inclusion on their mailing list.

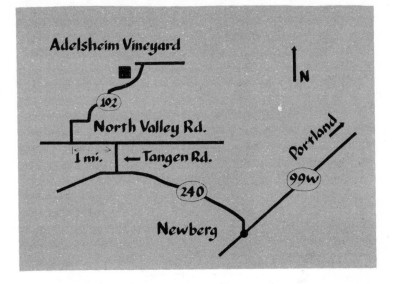

ADELSHEIM VINEYARD

David and Ginny Adelsheim are the owners and operators of one of Oregon's more innovative wineries. To prepare for the wine business, Adelsheim worked with David Lett during one of Eyrie's crushes, researched French and German viticulture and winemaking texts to gain a broader perspective than that offered by the teachings of the University of California at Davis, and studied and worked in France at the Lycee Viticole in Beaune.

Adelsheim talks not only of the future of his own winery, but of the future and destiny of the Oregon wine industry. On behalf of the Oregon Winegrowers Association, Adelsheim researched and petitioned the Federal Government for "viticultural area" designations for Oregon's Umpqua and Willamette Valleys. Oregon, he believes, will increasingly become one of America's most important premium wine producing regions as consumers become better educated to the higher acidity and more delicate and complex flavors of European and Oregon wines. But the process will be gradual, and Adelsheim's first Chardonnays and Pinot Noirs were made in a rounder, lower acid style to satisfy current consumer predelections.

The Adelsheims.

Pinot Noir is itself a wine that does not readily find a frame of reference in the popular American palate. French Burgundy has become so costly and unreliable that few Americans are familiar with the taste of good Pinot Noir. Adelsheim points out that Cabernet Sauvignon, the American standard frame of reference for red wines, is a much different kind of wine. Cabernet is strongly and distinctively flavored, striking the palate immediately with a highly defined taste. Pinot Noir, on the other hand, does not have such a readily recognizable taste, but rather unfolds on the palate in manifold nuances. In Adelsheim's view, an important aspect of wine tasting often ignored by Americans is the feel of a wine in the mouth. Fine Pinot Noir has a distinctive velvety feel—it is what Adelsheim calls a textural wine.

In addition to the standard Oregon grape varieties, Pinot Noir, Chardonnay, and Riesling, Adelsheim is also working with Pinot Gris and Sauvignon Blanc, and more recently, the true Gamay grape of Beaujolais, a variety very different from the misnamed Gamay Beaujolais clone of Pinot Noir. When the Adelsheims started making wine, Oregon grapes were in short supply, so they purchased Merlot and Semillon from south-central Washington, two varieties that are not well suited to the Willamette Valley. Although ample Oregon grapes are now available, the Washington Merlot

26

and Semillon have become so popular that the Adelsheims have decided to continue making them.

A broker for French oak barrels, Adelsheim has experimented with the effects of six different French oaks on the flavors of Pinot Noir and Chardonnay. Adelsheim prefers the tighter grained Allier and Vosges oak for Pinot Noir, and Limousin and Never for Chardonnay.

In his experience, Limousin accentuates the wine's acidity, offering pleasant, lemony qualities, though at the expense of some tendency toward bitter flavors. Never, on the other hand, brings out the softer, rounder qualities of the wine while playing down the acidity and any bitter tendencies.

Barrel staves are bent by either steaming, toasting over oak fires, or, occasionally, a combination of both methods. The fire bent barrels have always shown the best, and for Pinot Noir, Adelsheim prefers a particularly heavy toast.

The Adelsheim home and winery is a single, beautifully integrated structure. The winery, equipped for Adelsheim's 15,000 gallon annual production, occupies primarily the lower half of the building, and is partially underground. The view from the living room window is of the lush vineyard and the expansive valley below. Ginny's artwork graces the Adelsheim home as well as the labels for their wine.

ESTATE BOTTLED
Willamette Valley
CABERNET SAUVIGNON
1980
alcohol 12.4% by volume
produced and bottled by Alpine Vineyards, Alpine, Oregon
BW-OR-79

Alpine Vineyards
Founded 1980
Route 2, Box 173-D, Monroe, Oregon 97456
(503) 424-5851

Most Sundays, Noon to 5 PM.

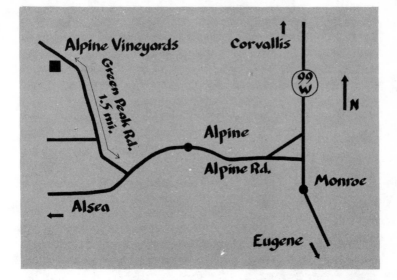

ALPINE VINEYARDS

Overlooking the lush vineyards and expansive valley below is the towering, modern, "passive solar" structure that is the Alpine Vineyards winery and the home of Dan and Christine Jepsen. Conveniently, the best sites for vineyards are also the best sites for solar homes. The hillside site, facing due south, is above the cooling temperature inversions and fogs of the valley floor. The grassy slopes and scattered oak trees confirm that this is a warmer, drier microclimate—warm enough, in fact, that Jepsen has five acres of Cabernet Sauvignon as well as the more typical Oregon plantings of Pinot Noir, Riesling, and Chardonnay.

Jepsen does not expect to produce a great Cabernet every year. As in Bordeaux, the most famous region for Cabernet Sauvignon, cooler years will yield lighter wines, but in the best years, when the grapes become fully ripe after a long period of maturation, the wines will be deep, complex, and long lived. Alpine's Cabernets are typically harvested in mid-November, fermented in stainless steel tanks, and aged in a combination of French and American oak barrels. Alpine's Cabernet grapes have moderate acidity, and Jepsen does not usually put his Cabernet Sauvignon

29

Christine and Dan Jepsen.

through a secondary malolactic fermentation that would further reduce the wine's acidity.

The Cabernet Sauvignon and Pinot Noir are fermented at 70 to 75 degrees, a moderately cool fermentation temperature for red wines. Although higher fermentation temperatures are sometimes thought to extract more from the grape, Alpine's fermentation is quite lengthy, lasting about two weeks. Each day for the first week, more grapes are harvested and added to the tank, thereby perpetuating the fermentation and prolonging the length of time the grapes are in contact with the skins.

The Pinot Noir is innoculated for malolactic fermentation during the final stages of the primary fermentation, and then racked into Allier and Limousin oak barrels for aging. In Riesling, the goal is not a heavy extract from the grape, but the preservation of delicate fruit esters. To achieve this, Alpine's Riesling is fermented at a cool

45 degrees for six to eight weeks. Alpine's Chardonnay is fermented in small stainless steel tanks at around 65 degrees, then aged in a combination of Limousin and Never oak barrels. It is usually not put through a secondary malolactic fermentation.

Alpine is one of the few Oregon wineries that is entirely estate bottled. Jepsen feels that eighty percent of a wines quality comes from the vineyard, and growing all of one's own grapes is one way to insure control over that eighty percent.

Alpine's grapes grow on their own rootstocks, but Jepsen has plantings of phylloxera resistant native American rootstocks for grafting, in case this dreaded root louse should ever invade Oregon.

The vineyard soil is a Jory clay loam running fifty feet to rock, interrupted only by occasional stretches of shallow Bellpine. The vineyard is not irrigated. Twenty acres are now in vine, and there is room for future expansion.

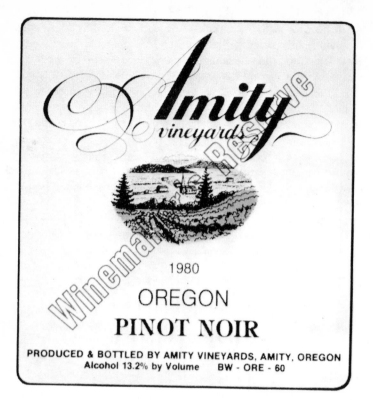

Amity vineyards

1980

OREGON
PINOT NOIR

PRODUCED & BOTTLED BY AMITY VINEYARDS, AMITY, OREGON
Alcohol 13.2% by Volume   BW - ORE - 60

Amity Vineyards
Founded 1976
Route 1, Box 348-B, Amity, Oregon 97101
(503) 835-2362

Daily, Noon to 5 PM, June through September; Saturdays and Sundays, Noon to 5 PM, October through May. Closed December 24 through January 31.

Oregon Winetasting Room at the Lawrence Gallery
9 miles southwest of McMinnville on Highway 18.
(503) 843-3787
Daily, Noon to 5 PM.

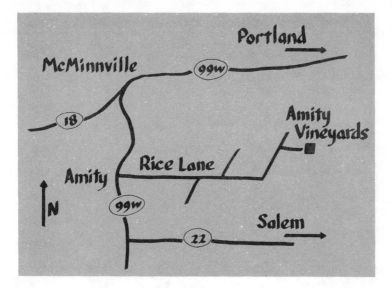

AMITY VINEYARDS

Myron Redford, Amity's winemaker, and one of the principal owners, did not set out to be an Oregon winegrower. First attracted to winemaking through part-time work at Washington's Associated Vintners winery, Redford intended to build a winery near Port Townsend, in western Washington, and like Associated Vintners, make wine from Washington grapes grown east of the Cascade Mountains.

While planning his winery, Redford learned of a vineyard for sale near Amity, Oregon, 45 miles southwest of Portland. Redford abandoned his plans for a Washington winery, and in 1974, formed a partnership and purchased the vineyard. A winery was built in 1976, and wine production began that year.

In the early years, Amity became best known for Pinot Noir Nouveau, a wine made predominantly from Washington grapes, and fermented by the carbonic maceration process. Patterned after the French Beaujolais Nouveau, the wine is meant to be consumed before the next vintage and enjoyed for its fresh, fruity qualities. Dry Riesling and Gewurztraminer also became Amity trademarks,

Myron Redford.

but none of these wines reflected the driving interest of Amity's winemaker.

From the beginning, Redford wanted Amity to be known for its Pinot Noir, not the "nouveau," but oak aged Pinot Noir from Oregon grapes. It was his interest in this wine that caused him to radically alter his plans and come to Oregon. In 1977, a very poor year for Oregon Pinot Noir, Redford succeeded in making an excellent wine, but in such miniscule quantity, 302 bottles, that it was scarcely available commercially. The following year, Redford made more good Pinot Noir, but held most of it back for four years before release.

Widespread recognition of Amity Pinot Noir was late in coming, but come it did. In an extensive tasting of more than 180 American Pinot Noirs, Amity's 1978 Winemaker's Reserve was one of only eleven given an outstanding rating by *Vintage Magazine's* tasting panel.

In recent vintages, Redford has released two barrel aged Pinot Noirs each year, one for more current consumption, and one intended for, and often needing, longer aging. Amity's "house style," therefore, encompasses a wide range, but Redford's preferences are most reflected in the wines intended for longer aging—fairly tannic, full-bodied wines with a sturdy acid armature.

Although Redford now favors blending the different lots, in 1977, from Oregon grapes, Redford separately bottled Pinot Noir from the Gamay and Wadenswil clones. True to traditional conceptions about the clones, the Gamay was lighter and higher in acid, the Wadenswil more flavorful and intense.

Subsequent years, however, have not always proved the common conceptions. The Gamay, particularly in warmer years, has produced wines with a depth and intensity contradicting its heritage. Much of Redford's Gamay, however, comes from older vines, a testimony to the tenet that vine age is an important factor in the quality of Pinot Noir. Redford believes that Pinot Noir does not even begin hitting stride until its sixth or seventh leaf—a point worthy of note, considering that the very oldest Willamette Valley Pinot Noir vines are not yet two decades old, and most, far younger.

In 1978, Myron Redford's brother, Steve, joined Amity to help with winemaking operations. Steve Redford, in addition to his work with Amity wines, purchases Washington and Oregon Cabernet Sauvignon and Merlot grapes for release under his own label, Redford Cellars. The wines are available only in very small quantities.

Amity operates a tasting room in the Lawrence Art Gallery in Bellevue, Oregon, nine miles south of McMinnville, on Highway 18, a major route to the Oregon coast. Wines from many Oregon wineries are available for tasting and purchase. The tasting room is open daily, from Noon to 5 PM.

Amity produces 15,000 gallons annually. Expansion to 20,000 gallons is planned. Redford keeps a mailing list for announcement of new releases, and the dates and times for Amity's two annual Solstice Wine Festivals.

Sauvignon Blanc
Oregon's Umpqua Valley

ALCOHOL 12% BY VOLUME

PRODUCED AND BOTTLED BY
BJELLAND VINEYARDS
ROSEBURG, OREGON

Bjelland Vineyards
Founded 1969
Bjelland Vineyards Lane, Roseburg, Oregon 97470
(503) 679-6950

Daily, 11 AM to 5 PM, September through May; daily, 10 AM to 5 PM, June through August.

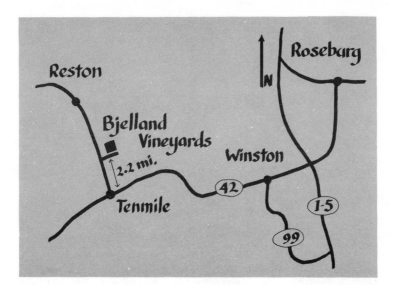

BJELLAND VINEYARDS

Located not far from Wildlife Safari, a popular tourist attraction, Bjelland Vineyards is just off Highway 42, one of the main routes from Interstate 5 to the Oregon coast. The winery and vineyards are at the base of Bjelland Rock, the highest mountain in the area, and perhaps the most distinctive landmark of any Northwest winery. According to Bjelland, the mountain was formed about a billion years ago at the end of what was then a glacial stream.

After many years in Los Angeles working in the public relations field, Bjelland sought a complete reversal in lifestyle, and eventually came to settle in this rural area of Oregon near Roseburg. His striped bib overalls have become a trademark, and bespeak the way of life he had sought, and now lives. After more than a decade, Bjelland still believes that it is the best life. In Paul Bjelland, the romance of winemaking has grown deep roots.

The winery and vineyards are wholly owned by the Bjellands. Although they have received offers for additional financial backing, the Bjellands prefer the independence of sole ownership. Partially because of this decision, an intimate, corresponsive relation-

Paul Bjelland.

ship has developed between the Bjellands and the rural lifestyle, each shaping and nurturing the other.

At one time, Bjelland wines were marketed in a number of states, including New York. The wines sold out rapidly, and the Bjellands found it was unnecessary to have such a widely based market. As a result, Bjelland wines are now available only at the winery and a few shops and stores in Oregon. Four thousand gallons are produced each year.

One of the new era pioneers, Bjelland's first decade of winemaking in Oregon was spent not only establishing the viability of his own winery, but as a corollary, the viability of the Oregon wine industry itself. The first years at Bjelland were devoted to breaking new ground—both figuratively and literally. In 1968, Bjelland founded the Oregon Winegrowers Association, and two years later, the first Oregon wine festival.

Bjelland wines are characterized by a light, easily palatable style. In addition to the traditional vinifera grape bottlings, Bjelland makes a woodruff flavored May Wine and several fruit and berry wines. In 1982, the Bjellands began giving additional emphasis to dry and semi-dry berry wines. In all, the Bjellands make fifteen different wines. All the wines, including the berry wines, are aged, at least in part, in American oak, though the older barrels Bjelland uses for aging do not impart a pronounced oak character.

The true Riesling grape is known by several names. Oregon law requires the wine to be designated by the name White Riesling, but because Bjelland had, for many years, labeled his wine Johannisberg Riesling, he has been allowed to continue that usage, and Bjelland Vineyards is the only Oregon winery allowed to use the Johannisberg Riesling name on its label.

At Bjelland, vine rows are 12 feet apart, and within the rows, vines are planted every eight feet. Although standard Oregon practice dictates much closer spacing to achieve the best grape quality and consistent crop yields, Bjelland believes that his wider spacing is best, reducing moisture and mildew problems, and easing tractor work.

The Bjellands and Bjelland winery epitomize country living. The surrounding countryside is attractive, and for those wishing to pick up a bottle or two of Bjelland wine for an afternoon outing, there are picnic areas and county parks nearby. Bjelland is also opening an Oregon Tasting Room at Bandon By the Sea, as well as a French restaurant, Zee Spendide, and a sidewalk cafe.

1982

CHATEAU BENOIT

OREGON WHITE RIESLING
Dry and distinctive

Produced and bottled by Château Benoît, Carlton, Oregon (BW-OR 80)
Alcohol 11.0% by volume

Chateau Benoit Winery
Founded 1979
Route 1, Box 29B-1, Mineral Springs Road,
Carlton, Oregon 97111
(503) 864-2991 or 864-3666

Saturday and Sunday, Noon to 5 PM.

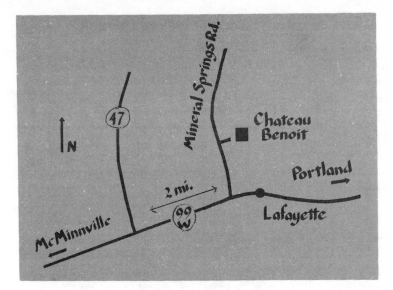

CHATEAU BENOIT WINERY

In 1972, Fred and Mary Benoit planted ten acres of grapes near Veneta, a small community in Lake County, just west of Eugene, in the southern Willamette Valley. What began as an investment and hobby, a diversion from Fred Benoit's medical practice, has evolved into a major enterprise.

The northern Willamette Valley is the center of Oregon's winegrowing industry. When the time came for expansion, the Benoits found the land and the community of winegrowers and winegrowing traditions they were seeking near McMinnville in the northern Willamette. Forty acres are now in vine, twenty at the Veneta site and twenty near McMinnville.

Although the general climatic conditions are similar in the Eugene and McMinnville areas, individual microclimates can vary widely. The Benoit's Veneta site is a benchland, and the soil is a rich, deep, silty loam called Salkum. It is a cool microclimate, subject to a ground frost in the spring that can be particularly damaging to young vines. In cool years, the vineyard may receive only 1,700 to 1,800 heat units. The site near McMinnville is quite different. The soil is Willakenzie, and the microclimate is one of the

41

Mary and Fred Benoit.

warmest and sunniest in the McMinnville area, receiving 2,500 to 2,700 heat units in warmer years, according to Benoit. Situated on a hillside, air movement is good, and spring frost is not a problem.

Benoit prefers the cooler Veneta site for his Pinot Noir. The new vineyards near McMinnville are all planted to white varieties, including ten acres of Muller-Thurgau, Oregon's largest single planting of this variety, a genetic cross of Riesling and Sylvaner producing a Riesling-like wine much in the style of the popular and ubiquitous Liebfraumilch from Germany. The Benoits like the grape, and will be planting additional acreage.

Interest in Muller-Thurgau is indicative of Chateau Benoit's "house style," a style that emphasizes the delicate fruit of the grape and a commitment to a winemaking approach typified by Germany and Switzerland. It is not surprising then that Chateau Benoit's first winemaker, Max Zellweger, was a native Swiss and a graduate of the College of Technology, Viticulture, and Horticulture in Wadenswil, Switzerland. Zellweger has since left Chateau Benoit to become winemaker for a new large Washington winery, F.W. Langguth.

Rich Cushman is Benoit's new winemaker. A native Oregonian, Cushman received a Masters degree in enology from U.C.

Davis, worked one crush with Trefethen in California, and then left to work for a year in the Rheinpfalz region of Germany for the respected winegrowing firm of Burklin-Wolf. Cushman joined Chateau Benoit in March of 1982.

Although the general style of German and Swiss wines are similar, winemaking methods sometimes differ. In making a white wine with some residual sugar, such as Riesling, the Swiss typically stop fermentation when the desired sweetness is reached. According to Cushman, typical German practice would call for use of a "sweet reserve," completely fermenting the must until it is dry, then adding unfermented grape juice until the desired sweetness is obtained. This method offers the winemaker additional flexibility by allowing comparative tastings of small test batches before making the final blend. Because some of the grape juice is not subject to the flavor transformations of fermentation, it can be expected that there would be subtle differences in taste from a wine that does not have unfermented grape juice added after fermentation. Both methods, nevertheless, suit the Chateau Benoit "house style."

Fermentation temperatures for white wines are kept low to emphasize the delicate fruit flavors, and no white wines, including Chardonnay, are aged in oak. Chateau Benoit produces some wines from Washington grapes. The Washington Riesling is made in a sweeter style than the Oregon Riesling. Washington Sauvignon Blanc has proven very successful and popular for the Benoits, and there are plans to plant the grape in their own Oregon vineyards.

The Benoits' son, Mark, graduated from Fresno State in viticulture, and now runs a vineyard management consulting service in the Willamette Valley, managing, among his accounts, the vineyards of Chateau Benoit. The Benoit vineyards are going to a vine pruning method that uses four canes per vine instead of the more conventional two. This method will increase the number of buds per square foot, and hopefully increase the yield without the necessity of increasing the number of vines per acre.

Chateau Benoit wines are available in Oregon, Washington, and Idaho, and will become available in more states as the Benoit vineyards mature and production increases beyond the present 20,000 gallons a year.

côte des colombes

V I N E Y A R D

oregon
cabernet sauvignon

produced and bottled by côte des colombe vineyard
bw · or · 68   banks, oregon
ALCOHOL 12% BY VOLUME

Cote des Colombes Vineyard
Founded 1977
P.O. Box 266, Banks, Oregon 97106
(503) 324-0855 or 646-1223

Saturday and Sunday, 1 PM to 5 PM. Closed during January.

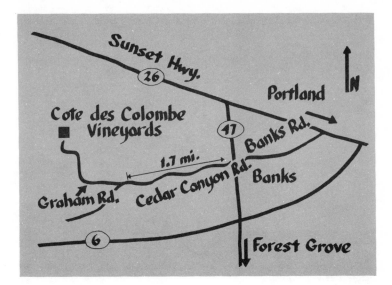

COTE DES COLOMBES VINEYARD

Cote des Colombes is one of the smaller Northwest wineries open to the public. The winery name is French for "Hill of the Doves," and is derived from the French spelling of Joe Coulombe's surname. A home winemaker, and formerly the owner of two retail wine shops in the Portland area, Coulombe sold his businesses to begin the winery.

The vineyard is presently very modest, consisting of five acres of vines. More acreage is being planted, but until the vineyards are more fully developed, most of Cote des Colombes' wines will be made from grapes purchases from other Oregon growers. A few grapes will also be purchased from Washington growers.

Coulombe has been one of the chief promoters of Oregon oak (*Quercus garryana*) for wine aging. Coulombe cites controlled studies at the University of California at Davis comparing the taste of Oregon oak with French and other oaks traditionally used for aging wine. Oregon oak showed very well, and was thought to be quite similar to the French oaks.

Cote des Colombes.

Because of a shortage of cured Oregon oak and difficulty finding reliable coopers to make a barrel or two for experimental purposes, Coulombe first tested the flavors of the oak by putting oak chips into stainless steel barrels. But in 1982, the first Oregon oak barrels were delivered to the winery, and are now used for aging some of Coulombe's Pinot Noir.

In 1982, the winery buildings were remodeled and expanded to make way for stainless steel tanks and an oak barrel aging room. The old barn that had stood on the property collapsed in a powerful windstorm the previous November, and the beautiful weathered boards from the 115 year old structure conveniently provided decorative siding for the new buildings.

The principal wine varieties produced by Cote des Colombes include Riesling, Chardonnay, Gewurztraminer, Pinot Noir, Cabernet Sauvignon, and Chenin Blanc. Emphasis on these latter two varieties is unusual for an Oregon winery.

Cabernet Sauvignon and Chenin Blanc require warmer and longer growing seasons, a combination not always found in the Willamette Valley's cooler vintages. The first releases of these wines were made from Washington grapes, but Coulombe is beginning to make them from Oregon grapes. The first estate grown Cabernet Sauvignon was produced in 1982.

Cote des Colombes hosts three wine functions each year, the Renaissance Wine Festival in June, a barrel tasting in July, and the Anniversary Open House on Thanksgiving weekend.

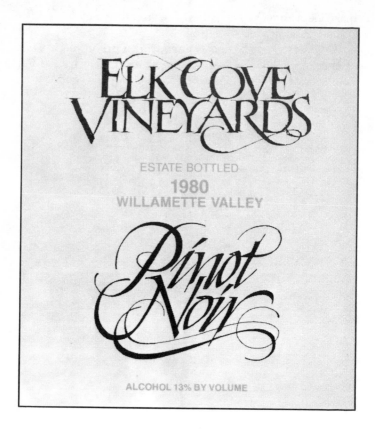

Elk Cove Vineyards
Founded 1977
Route 3, Box 23, Gaston, Oregon 97119
(503) 985-7760

Daily, Noon to 5 PM. Closed Easter, Thanksgiving, and Christmas.

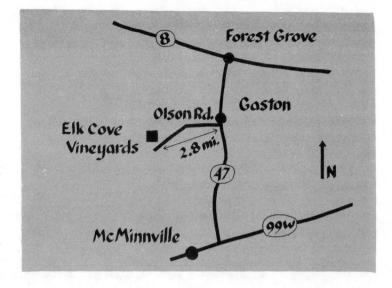

ELK COVE VINEYARDS

Elk Cove Vineyards is one of Oregon's most interesting and successful new wineries. Solely owned and operated by the Campbell family, Pat and Joe Campbell, wife and husband, equally share winemaking duties and decision making. The Campbells' 136 acre estate is located near a hilltop outside of Gaston, Oregon. Seventy acres are suitable for vineyards. Twenty-four acres are now planted, and expansion is planned. 1977 was Elk Cove's first commercial crush. Rapidly outgrowing their first winery building, a large, modern winery and tasting room was built in 1981. Twenty thousand gallons of wine are produced annually.

Many premium American wineries are, to a degree, moving away from strict adherence to the methodologies and mind set of the University of California at Davis, and looking again toward European winegrowing practices. Because Oregon has a climate more generally similar to some of Europe's premium growing regions, the state has more to gain in the new world's return to its viticultural roots. It is not, however, a return to unscientific practices. Europe has a long tradition of rigorous and comprehensive inquiry into the science and art of grape growing and winemaking in cooler climates.

49

Joe and Pat Campbell.

In Oregon, Elk Cove is among those wineries most oriented toward European methods.

This is not to say that the teachings of U.C. Davis are ignored or rejected out of hand. Pat Campbell regards the short courses she attended at the U.C. Davis as a valuable source of winemaking information, but the California school is, understandably, directed more toward the problems and interests of California winemaking, problems and interests that frequently differ from those of Oregon winemakers. California winegrowers typically confront excessive crop yields, and grapes with high sugars and low acids. Oregon winegrowers typically confront light yields, low sugars, and high acids.

In Europe, vines are often planted much more densely than is common in California. Many believe that increasing the number of vines per acre insures more consistent yields at favorable sugar and acid levels. Elk Cove's vines are planted six feet apart, in rows seven feet apart, a density of 1,054 vines per acre. Domestic farm machinery cannot cope with these narrow rows, and the Campbells are forced to put up with the scarcity of parts and repair service for their 48 inch wide Italian tractor. Because each vine must be pruned, trained, and cared for, the expense of this higher density planting is considerably greater.

It is commonly believed that increasing the vine's foliage increases its capacity to produce and ripen grapes, but as European studies show, this is only partially true. After approximately the fourteenth leaf on the main shoots and the fourth leaf on the lateral shoots, nutrient production merely supports foliage and no longer benefits the grapes. Elk Cove and other Oregon growers have taken to a practice called hedging, trimming vine shoots to benefit grape production and ripening, a time consuming procedure, and an added expense.

Traditional methods are applied in the winery as well as the vineyard. The Chardonnay is fermented in French oak barrels. During one vintage, the Campbells had insufficient cooperage to ferment all their Chardonnay in oak, and some of the wine was fermented in stainless steel barrels. After two weeks, when fermentation was completed, both the oak fermented and stainless steel fermented wines were put into oak barrels for aging. After nine months, the Campbells report that the wines were distinctly different. Although the oak fermented wine did not have a stronger oak flavor, it was fuller and more complex. This firsthand comparative experience made the Campbells strong advocates of oak barrel fermentation.

Before pressing and fermentation begin, Elk Cove's Chardonnay is left on its skins and stems for 12 to 18 hours. The Campbells ferment their Chardonnay with the Montrachet strain of yeast, a strain that has a reputation for producing fuller, richer wines, but at increased risk of the undesireable byproduct, hydrogen sulfide. To avoid the problem of hydrogen sulfide, the Campbells treat their grapes with little or no sulfur, and their Chardonnay benefits from the Montrachet yeast without suffering its undesireable byproduct.

Elk Cove's Pinot Noirs have a style distinctively and successfully their own. Pinot Noir is Elk Cove's premier wine. The Pinot Noir is fermented in 200 gallon bins, and the cap of pulp and skins is punched down three to four times a day. According to the year, varying amounts of stems are included during fermentation. In less ripe years, the stems are green and fewer are used. After fermentation is completed, the pulp, skins, and stems are left to macerate in the must for five days. The wine is then pressed, and racked into Allier oak barrels.

Grapes are highly sensitive to small changes in growing environment. The grapes Elk Cove purchases from other growers in the northern Willamette Valley are fermented and bottled separately. Differences in soil, climate, and growing methods are brought more clearly into focus when these different grapes are made into wine by the same winemaker. Comparison of Elk Cove Pinot Noirs from their own estate, and from the Wind Hill Vineyard in the Forest Grove area west of Portland is a case in point. Both vineyards were planted the same year, to the same clone of Pinot Noir, obtained from the same source. The Wind Hill Vineyard is planted in a clay shot soil, the Elk Cove Vineyard in a sandier soil called Willakenzie Silty Loam. The Wind Hill Vineyard has had lighter yields. The site is warmer, and ripens one to two weeks ahead of Elk Cove's vineyard. The Wind Hill Pinot Noirs tend to be more tannic and display a more forward fruit intensity. The estate grown Pinot Noirs tend to be rounder and earthier. Both are very good—and very different.

Even minute variations in growing environment can make a difference. The Elk Cove vineyard has a very slight roll in the land that encompasses only a few rows of vines. Grapes from these rows are slightly riper and more intense than the rest, and in the best years, these grapes become part of the foundation for Elk Cove's "reserve" Pinot Noir.

The hard realities of economic necessity weigh heavily on the winegrower. Winegrowers need a grape that produces a reliable crop, and can be turned into wine and released soon after the vintage, in short, a cash flow wine to keep the home fires burning and the bankers happy. In Oregon, for this purpose, Riesling is the grape of choice. Not only is Riesling a good "safety grape," it also produces good wine. The ultimate Rieslings, however, are made from botrytised grapes, grapes that have been infected with the *Botrytis cinerea* mold in such a way that the grape essences are highly concentrated. But if conditions are not ideal, the botrytis becomes gray rot, and the crop can be damaged or lost. Oregon 's frequently rainy falls make botrytised wines a very risky business, and few winegrowers are willing to subject their "safety wine" to such a risk.

Elk Cove is an exception. In years when conditions are favorable, the vines are left unsprayed, and the botrytis is allowed to develop. In the best years, in German fashion, a Riesling is made from individually selected clusters of the most botrytised grapes. These wines are expensive to produce. In addition to the risk, twice the picking time is needed, and the grapes, shriveled from the botrytis, yield much less juice. Toward the end of harvest, after many nights of little sleep, winegrowers do not look forward to additional risk, worry, and time consuming tasks, but the Campbell's botrytised Rieslings have rewarded them well, and have become benchmarks in the exploration of Riesling's potential in Oregon.

Elk Cove has grown considerably since its first years of production, but it still retains a personal and personable flavor that makes it a pleasure to visit. The attractive tasting room overlooks the vineyards below. In the spring, Roosevelt elk meander through the hillside.

The Eyrie Vineyards
Founded 1966
P.O. Box 204, Dundee, Oregon 97115
935 East 10th Avenue, McMinnville, Oregon 97128
(503) 472-6315 or 864-2410

Eyrie is not open to the public, except for the annual Thanksgiving Weekend Tasting, occasional special events, and by appointment. Write to be included on the mailing list.

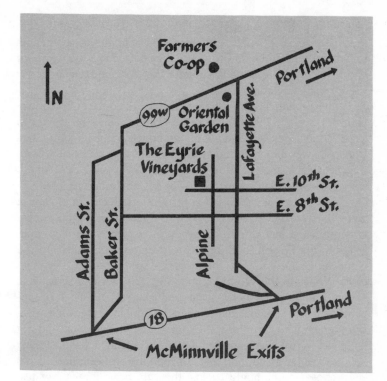

THE EYRIE VINEYARDS

David Lett is one of the true pioneers of Oregon's wine industry. Although he came to Oregon in 1965, four years after Hillcrest's Richard Sommer had settled in the Roseburg area, Lett was the first winemaker in recent times to grow vinifera grapes in the Willamette Valley area near Portland, and moreover, the first Oregon winemaker choosing to focus his efforts on a red wine—Pinot Noir.

With a degree in viticulture from the University of California at Davis, and some practical California winemaking experience, Lett began looking for an area to grow the Burgundian grape varieties, Pinot Noir and Chardonnay. Then as now, successful California Pinot Noirs were rare, and although Chardonnay is now perhaps California's best wine, in the 1960's, California Chardonnays were picked too early, saw little or no oak, and were for the most part unexceptional. With this frame of reference, Lett came to Oregon, passed by the Roseburg area believing it too warm for Pinot Noir, and chose the Willamette Valley's Dundee Hills as the site for his vineyards.

In selecting this site, Lett was not only singular in his conviction, but virtually solitary. Everyone from his Davis professors to local farmers advised against his enterprise, and Oregon State University was then recommending *Vitis labrusca* as the only commercially viable species. Most painfully, years would pass after the first vines were planted before his beliefs could be validated.

Lett's interest in Pinot Noir proved farsighted. Pinot Noir, a grape that rarely does well outside of Burgundy, is Oregon's stellar wine grape, a fact confirmed by the now famous tastings published in the French food and wine magazine, *Gault/Millau, Le Nouveau Guide.* In 1979, the magazine sponsored an "Olympics of the Wines of the World," pitting the 330 best of 586 original entries from 33 of the worlds wine producing regions. To the disappointment of many, including Robert J. Drouhin of the well-known Burgundian wine firm Joseph Drouhin, the French wines did not do as well as had been expected. Drouhin contended that the tasting had been unbalanced, and that less than the best Burgundies had been chosen to compete against the very best "foreign" wines. Drouhin proposed a rematch, pitting the top-scoring foreign Pinot Noirs against Burgundies selected from the Drouhin cellars.

On January 8, 1980, under the supervision of M. Jacques Puisais, President of the International Union of Enologists, twenty French, English, and American wine judges of considerable repute conducted a formal tasting of the wines. Drouhin's 1959 Chambolle-Musigny was the first place wine. In third place was his 1961 Chambertin Clos-de-Beze. The second place wine, two tenths of a point out of first, was the 1975 Eyrie Vineyards South Block Reserve from Oregon.

After fifteen years of pioneer adversity, the results of the *Gault/Millau* tasting were sweet indeed. This landmark tasting not only brought Eyrie instant recognition, it helped bring well-deserved and long overdue attention to the Oregon wine industry.

Lett believes that more than any other variety, Pinot Noir is a winegrower's, and above all, a winemaker's grape. Cabernet Sauvignon has a strong and immediate varietal profile, but Pinot Noir is delicate, elusive, and subtle. Grown in less than ideal conditions, the varietal character disappears completely, yet this sub-

David Lett.

tle quality makes the grape highly responsive to slight changes in growing conditions and winemaking methods. More than any other variety, Pinot Noir reflects the winemaker's style, the winemaker's art.

Eyrie Pinot Noirs are reflective of Lett's preferences and predilections. Though his now famous 1975 South Block Pinot Noir is one of his best wines and one of his "biggest," Lett disparages the preoccupation with "big" wines. The strength of the '75 is not its "power," but its elegance and complex flavors. Of Burgundies Lett tends to prefer those with perfumed finesse rather than the bigger, and, to his taste, sometimes more clumsy wines of the northernmost Cote de Nuits.

Lett uses no stems in fermentation, and in general, minimizes tannin, believing that too much tannin interferes with the character of the wine. Lett holds that if Pinot Noir has adequate acid structure, tannins are largely unnecessary for aging. Eyrie's Pinot Noir is fermented in small, four-foot-square bins. Temperatures reach the high eighties. At the height of fermentation, Lett sleeps in the winery, and punches down the fermenting cap of skins and pulp every two hours around the clock. It is Lett's contention that frequent punching-down is critical for maceration of the must and extraction of flavors. The Pinot Noir undergoes malolactic fermentation, and is bottled after 14 to 23 months in French oak. Some special reserve Pinot Noirs may occasionally spend as long as 30 months in oak.

Most of Eyrie's Pinot Noir is the Wadenswil clone. Lett concedes that clonal differences exist, but emphasizes that other factors are far more significant. Distinctive character tends to show itself as vines grow older. With age, the vines, and so too their grapes, are subject to transformation. It is in keeping with the elusive nature of Pinot Noir that attempts to capture clonal differences with definitive statements is a tenuous proposition at best.

Eyrie Pinot Noirs are not darkly colored wines. Lett decries the American, and particularly the West Coast, prejudice that high tannin, high alcohol, and inky color somehow equate with quality or longevity. Coloring constituents, essentially anthocyanins, do not necessarily correlate with flavoring constituents, yet when confronted with a row of glasses, a wine taster immediately looks to the darkest in expectation of finding "the best." Before even smelling or tasting the wine, his opinions, so to speak, are already colored. Relating a visit with Andre Noblet, winemaker for Burgundy's famed Romanee-Conti, Lett quotes him as saying, "Color in a beautiful wine is no more important than clothes on a beautiful woman."

Lett produces Chardonnay, another Burgundian grape variety, and a mainstay of the Oregon wine industry, but eschews Oregon's traditional third major variety, Riesling. Many feel that Riesling does not make a very good dry wine, but is at its best with some residual sugar. Lett, preferring to make dry wines, wines to go with food, has budded over nearly all his Riesling vines to another grape variety, Pinot Gris, a little-known white wine grape.

For years, Lett has produced miniscule quantities of Pinot Gris from a few experimental vines, and for years, he has been enamored with the grape variety and its wines. A direct relative of Pinot Noir, Pinot Gris is a viable alternative to Riesling. Riesling is popular with winegrowers because it consistently produces palatable wines, even in poor years. It requires no oak and no aging, and can be released soon after the vintage, providing much needed cash flow for the winegrower. Pinot Gris has these same attributes, but it is a good food wine as well.

Except for Chardonnay, virtually all white grape varieties grown in the Willamette Valley on a commercial scale are Germanic in style, Riesling or Riesling-like, floral varietals either directly or distantly related to Muscat, and best suited to a slightly sweet style.

Pinot Gris is different. At its worst, Pinot Gris can be a bit heavy and flat, with some bitterness in the finish. At its best, it is a crisp, full-bodied, flavorful wine of distinction. It is similar to its red cousin, Pinot Noir, in that it does not have a high varietal profile as does, for example, Cabernet Sauvignon or Sauvignon Blanc, but instead communicates its merit through a subtle interplay of flavors. Unlike Oregon Chardonnay, it is not temperamental, but ripens easily, reliably produces good crops, and is relatively easy to turn into good wine.

Lett, however, does not intend Pinot Gris as a replacement for Chardonnay. In his rendition, Pinot Gris is fermented in stainless steel, put through a malolactic fermentation, bottled without oak aging, and released soon after the vintage. Pinot Gris is the dry wine drinker's answer to Riesling, and in many ways, it is preferable to all but the better Oregon Chardonnays.

Two decades ago, Lett assumed the risk of pioneering Pinot Noir in Oregon's Willamette Valley. Two decades later, Lett is again subscribing to risk and committing himself to Pinot Gris, a direct relative of Pinot Noir. In partnership with an adjacent grower, John Schetky, Lett is committing fully half of his yearly wine production to this unknown and unrecognized grape. To a marketing consultant, his commitment would seem unwise at best, but two decades ago, his commitment to Oregon Pinot Noir was similarly foolish. If Pinot Gris does not become one of Oregon's major grape varieties, it will not be for lack of merit, and it will not be for lack of pioneering commitment.

Forgeron Vineyard
Founded 1977
89697 Sheffler Road, Elmira, Oregon 97437
(503) 935-1117 or 935-3530

Daily, Noon to 5 PM.

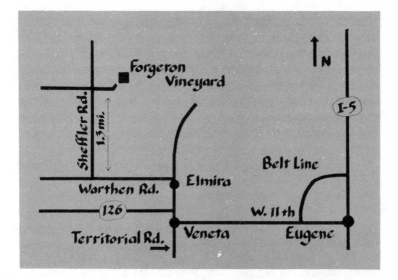

FORGERON VINEYARD

Climate measurements at Eugene suggest that this southern portion of the Willamette Valley is nearly identical to the northern Willamette near Portland. Such is not the case. The microclimates surrounding Eugene vary considerably, and some are warmer and otherwise differ significantly in character from the growing areas of the northern Willamette. Forgeron vineyard is one such microclimate.

The choice of Forgeron's vineyard location was no accident. In the late 1960's, an environmental impact study was conducted to evaluate the feasibility of a nuclear power plant near Eugene. The power plant was never built, but its latent legacy was a highly comprehensive source of climatological information. Taking advantage of this data, Lee and Linda Smith selected their vineyard site, and in 1972, planted their first grapes. Twenty acres are now in vine.

According to Smith, Forgeron has 55 more days of sunshine than Eugene, and seven to ten inches less rainfall. Although the days are warm, the nights are quite cool, a condition Smith feels is a key factor in the quality of his Pinot Noir and Cabernet Sauvignon, and also an important element in encouraging the growth of *Botrytis cinerea*, a mold that, under the right conditions, is responsible for special, sweet, white wines of exceptional quali-ty. Oregon vintages, like vintages of European winegrowing climates, vary much more than those of California. Smith reports that heat summation measurements in his vineyard have ranged from 2,000 to over 3,000, though "typical" years average 2,400 to 2,500.

In part because of this warmer microclimate, Forgeron is one of the few Oregon wineries pursuing Cabernet Sauvignon. Forgeron produces much more Pinot Noir than Cabernet Sauvignon, but the Cabernet is Smith's personal favorite. He reports that his Cabernet Sauvignon ripens well nearly every year. This is no great trick with small experimental plots producing low, non-commercial yields, but Smith's vines are generously cropped to a commercially viable four to five tons an acre.

Unlike most Oregon wineries, Forgeron produces only moderate amounts of Chardonnay. Smith thinks that the Chardonnay clones planted in Oregon are not the best for the climate, presenting countless problems in growing and ripening. Oregon State University is working with a number of Chardonnay clones, but Smith believes the development could take fifteen to twenty years.

Forgeron grows small amounts of Chenin Blanc, a late ripening grape. Although the Chenin Blanc barely ripens in most years, it lends itself well to the beneficial botrytis mold. Some Pinot Gris is also produced, made in both a dry and an unusual semi-dry style.

Forgeron's biggest planting is in Riesling, a grape that Smith ferments at very low temperatures, about 40 to 45 degrees, to preserve the delicate fruit esters of the grape. Smith has found that the standard strains of dried yeast do not work well at these temperatures, and he now imports live yeast cultures from France to do the job.

Several experiments with vine training and vine pruning are underway. One of the more interesting methods is the "Italian T." Four fruiting canes are allowed to grow vertically until they bend over into the rows from their own weight. Pruning is easy. Each season, the vines are clipped off at the top of their training wires. The remaining cane becomes a cordon, a permanent portion of the vine from which new canes grow each season. Not only does this method increase sun exposure, but the vines can be mechanically harvested. No Oregon winegrowers are mechanical-ly harvesting now, nor is there any immediate need for mechanical

Lee Smith.

harvesting, but if hand harvesting became too expensive or there were a labor shortage, the mechanical harvesting option would be desireable, and the "Italian T," with the canes and grapes hanging into the rows, is suited to the type of machinery that could be practical in Oregon—not the mechanical monsters that straddle entire vine rows, but smaller, less expensive machinery, harvesting one side of a row at a time, and capable of operating in hillier terrain.

Yearly production is about 10,000 gallons. Forgeron's first wines were fermented in the lower portion of the Smith's home. In 1981, the Smith's built a large winery with a production capacity of 25,000 gallons a year.

Glen Creek Winery
Founded 1982
6057 Orchard Heights Road N.W., Salem, Oregon 97304
(503) 371-WINE

Weekends, Noon to 5 PM from Memorial Day through Labor Day.
Other times by appointment.

GLEN CREEK WINERY

Founder of a leading southern California wine shop, Thomas Dumm was among the first few in the state to stock Northwest wines. In 1976, Dumm and his family left California for a better life style in Oregon. Settling in a rural area near Salem, Dumm planted a few grape vines and continued with his interest in home winemaking, a hobby that would soon to grow into a commercial enterprise.

Dumm prepared for winemaking on a commercial scale by attending a series of courses at the University of California at Davis. In 1982, Glen Creek had its first crush, 6,000 gallons of wine from Washington grapes. Dumm will gradually shift to Oregon grapes as growers are contracted and local vineyards mature. Glen Creek has the capacity to produce 10,000 gallons a year.

The original small family vineyard, planted to Chardonnay and Riesling, stands adjacent to the winery. In 1983, eight more acres were planted nearby. The new vines, mostly Gewurztraminer and Chardonnay, will be cordon pruned, a practice predominant in California, but rare in Oregon where vines are almost always cane pruned. With cordon pruning, the vines are left with perma-

65

Sylvia and Thomas Dumm.

nent lateral arms called cordons. In the spring, new growth emerges from these cordons. Although this vine training method is infrequent in cooler climates, cordon pruned vines are more easily maintained, and require less skilled labor and attention.

Dumm built Glen Creek's tasting room in the aging cellar so that visitors would not be isolated from the sights and smells of the winery, and just outside, tall, temperature controlled tanks glisten in the sun. Next to the tanks and vineyard, Dumm is building an arbor-covered picnic area.

HENRY ESTATE

OREGON
PINOT NOIR
1979

MADE ENTIRELY FROM PINOT NOIR GRAPE
PRODUCED AND BOTTLED BY HENRY WINERY, UMPQUA, OR
BONDED WINERY OR-74   ALCOHOL 13% BY VOLUME

Henry Winery
Founded 1978
P.O. Box 26, Highway 6, Umpqua, Oregon 97486
(503) 459-5120 or 459-3614

Daily, 11 AM to 5 PM.

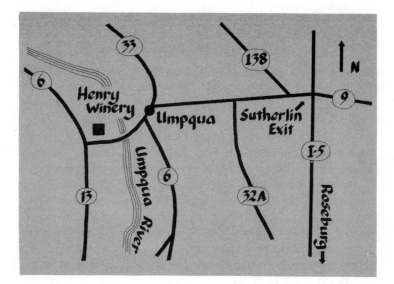

HENRY WINERY

The Henry Winery is a paradox, a winery firmly rooted in Oregon's rural, pioneering, winegrowing traditions, yet contrasting with, and contradicting, many of those same traditions. Scott Henry is the winery's founder. Henry became interested in wine from his close friend and colleague, Gino Zepponi, when they were both working for the same California engineering firm. Zepponi became the "Z" in California's ZD winery, and is now vice president of the large California sparkling wine producer, Domaine Chandon. In 1971, Henry and Zepponi came to Oregon to look at the prospects for winegrowing. In 1972, Henry left California and the engineering firm, moved to Oregon, and planted 12 acres of wine grapes in Oregon's Umpqua Valley.

Many of Oregon's winegrowers have come to the state from California, but Henry was not a newcomer. The Henry family has lived and ranched in the Umpqua Valley for over a hundred years. The family ranch and orchards are on bottomland near the Umpqua River, and it was here that Henry planted his grapes, thus immediately violating Oregon winegrowing traditions, and the fundamental tenet that Oregon vineyards should be planted on southerly slopes above the valley floor.

The soil is a Roseburg Sandy Loam, running fifteen feet to gravel. Skeptics believed that the flatland vineyards would not have enough air movement to dispel destructive spring frosts, would not be sunny or warm enough to ripen the grapes, and would produce mostly vegetation anyway, instead of producing grapes.

All these predictions proved wrong. The nearby Umpqua River protects the vines from frost. As the temperature approaches freezing, the moist, river air fogs up, protecting the vines from frost much in the same way that overhead sprinkler systems are used to create a moist heating-freezing shield around the vines. Over five years, the vineyard site has had an average of 2,200 heat units a year, and it so happens that, during the growing season, a cut in the Coast Range Mountains corresponds with the position of the setting sun, thus increasing the effective day length. Adequate grape sugars are not a problem.

The Henrys' decorative grape arbor consistently produced grapes every year, and Henry had little doubt that his vineyard would have a commercially viable grape yield. This proved more than true. In Oregon, three tons an acre is considered a good average yield for most grape varieties. Scott Henry's vineyards yield six to eight tons of Chardonnay and Pinot Noir per acre. Most feel that higher yields tend to dilute a wine's quality, but Henry maintains that after experimenting with a wide range of yields, six to eight tons results in the best wine. At lower yield levels, the "second crop," the late clusters of berries that do not fully ripen and are not picked for wine, appear to be ripe. Pickers, not readily able to distinguish the second crop from the regular crop, pick these grapes anyway, thus decreasing the quality of the wine. Because Henry's vineyards produce more than twice as much wine per acre as most Oregon vineyards, the winery is on more stable financial footing.

The type of wines the Henry Winery produces, however, presents an extra expense. The production of most Oregon wineries includes a substantial portion of a cash flow wine, usually Riesling. Although better with age, Rieslings can be released within six months of the harvest, offering immediate income, and clearing out storage and fermentation tanks for the next vintage. Henry produces no Riesling, and only small amounts of Gewurztraminer. Virtually all of Henry's production is in Chardonnay and Pinot Noir. The Henry winery, in fact, is one of the state's largest producers

Scott Henry.

of these wines, although many wineries have greater total wine production.

These factors dovetail into another unconventionality. Both Pinot Noir and Chardonnay are customarily aged in small oak barrels, and are not released for one to two or more years after the vintage. This requires an immense investment in cooperage. With rare exception, Oregon wineries use only the more expensive French oaks for aging. At three times the price of American oak, this seemed prohibitively expensive to Henry. His friend and consultant, Zepponi, urged Henry to use American oak cooperage, as is widespread practice in California. Zepponi insisted that consumer acceptance and competition awards would be no different than if French oak was used.

Zepponi proved correct, and the wines proved controversial. Henry prefers a riper, fuller style of wine. Because of this and the American oak, some critics have suggested Henry's wines more closely resemble the wines of California than the wines of Oregon. Others praise them as the best in the state. The wines are exceptionally well made, and their merit is a matter of preference.

Thirty-one acres are now in vine. Henry has the land to expand to several hundred acres, but little interest in growing that large. Yearly production is 15,000 gallons, an amount that will double as the vineyard matures.

71

1981

Hidden Springs

Oregon
White Riesling

PRODUCED AND BOTTLED BY
HIDDEN SPRINGS WINERY, INC.
AMITY, OREGON, U.S.A.
BW-OR-81

Alcohol 11.5% by Volume

Hidden Springs Winery
Founded 1980
Route 1, Box 252-B, Amity, Oregon 97101
(503) 835-2782, 581-2627, or 363-1295

Saturday, 11 AM to 5 PM; Sunday, Noon to 5 PM; March through November. Call for December hours.

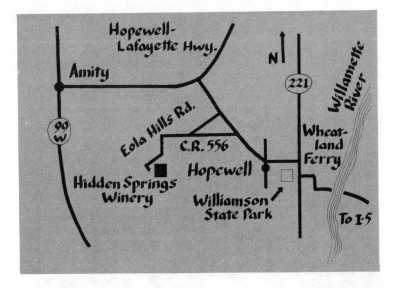

HIDDEN SPRINGS WINERY

Hidden Springs Winery is a corporation owned by two families from Salem, Don and Carolyn Byard and Al and Jo Alexanderson. Each family owns their own vineyard and sells grapes to the corporation. The Alexandersons' vineyard is near Salem , the Byards', northwest of Salem, in the Eola Hills between Amity and Hopewell. In all, twenty-seven acres are in vine and fifteen more will be planted within the next several years. The Byard vineyard is a former cherry and prune orchard, the remaining prune trees bringing in a steady income as the vines mature. Nearby, a former prune drying building has been converted into a winery.

Most of Oregon's climatological information comes from data gathered at airport weather stations, but since airports are usually in valleys, and vineyards are usually at higher elevations, on hillsides with southerly exposures, winegrowers have not had the benefit of reliable, basic information, much less information on the important subtleties, comparing, for example, the implications of a southwesterly exposure versus a southeasterly exposure, the effects of cloud cover at different points in the growing season, and so on. Byard is participating in an experimental program with Oregon State University to gather more accurate and useful data.

Al Alexanderson and Don Byard.

Thermographs have been placed at several vineyard locations in the Willamette Valley, including Byard's. Thermographs measure, automatically and continuously, temperature, humidity, and the intensity of the sunlight. Hidden Springs had its first commercial crush in 1980, a cool, wet, difficult year for most growers, and not the easiest rites of initiation for the beginning winegrower. Under less than ideal conditions, the success of Hidden Spring's first wines was an auspicious beginning. Riesling, Chardonnay, and Pinot Noir are the principal varieties.

When conversation turns to clonal selection, Pinot Noir is the grape that comes first to mind, but other varieties have clonal variants as well, though not to the same degree as Pinot Noir. As part of another experimental program, three different clones of Riesling are planted at the Eola site.

Small test plots of other grapes are grown as well. Sauvignon Blanc has proven particularly successful, and is the basis for the winery's blended white wine. Land near the winery building does not have the best exposure for a vineyard site, but Muller-Thurgau, a Riesling-like variety does well on such sites, and some may be planted.

Many Oregon wineries in the northern Willamette Valley, particularly newer wineries waiting for their vineyards to mature, purchase Washington grapes to supplement production. Hidden Springs makes wine only from Oregon grapes. Production, necessarily modest in the first years, will temporarily level off at 10,000 gallons annually.

1981

Hillcrest Vineyard

OREGON
WHITE RIESLING

alcohol 10.5 % by volume

PRODUCED & BOTTLED BY HILLCREST VINEYARD
ROSEBURG, OREGON   BONDED WINERY OR-44

Hillcrest Vineyard
Founded 1963
240 Vineyard Lane, Roseburg, Oregon 97470
(503) 673-3709

Daily, 10 AM to 5 PM.

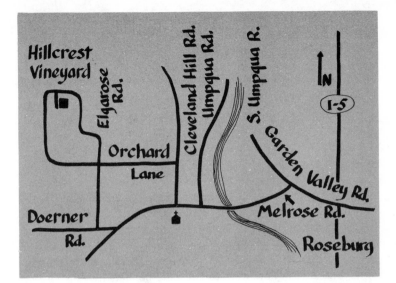

HILLCREST VINEYARD

In 1961, Richard Sommer bought acreage and planted wine grapes in Oregon's Umpqua Valley near Roseburg, and with that, became the proverbial father and founder of Oregon's wine industry.

Sommer studied agronomy and viticulture at the University of California at Davis, and after an intervening period, came to Oregon in search of a cooler winegrowing climate. Sampling some of the few vinifera grapes that were then growing in Oregon, Sommer was satisfied he had found the proper climate. Although there were remnants of earlier winegrowing efforts, when Sommer came to Oregon, there was virtually no precedent that would give him any assurance of success.

For the winegrowers that followed, Sommer not only provided direct assistance, but perhaps even more importantly, served as an example that commercial, premium, vinifera winegrowing in Oregon was not only possible, but viable. More than two decades have passed since Sommer came to Oregon. Although the state's wine industry has grown tremendously, and many wineries are vying for attention and recognition, for many years,

Sommer's Hillcrest Vineyard and premium Oregon wine were virtually synonymous.

The Hillcrest vineyard is 850 feet above sea level, higher and slightly cooler than any other winery in the Roseburg area, but very well suited to Riesling. Fully two thirds of Hillcrest's 30 acres are planted to the grape, and Hillcrest has made its reputation on Riesling wines. Ninety-five percent of the grapes for Hillcrest's 20,000 gallon annual production are grown in the vineyards surrounding the winery, each acre yielding an average of four to six tons of wine grapes.

Although Oregon is now known for several grape varieties, when Sommer pioneered this cooler grape growing region, Riesling, a well known, premium, cool climate grape, was the most logical choice, and today, Riesling is still the mainstay of the Oregon wine industry.

Nearly every Oregon winery releases Riesling soon after the vintage as a cash flow wine to keep the bankers away from the door. Most Oregon Riesling is purchased and consumed within a year of the vintage. Although a tasty wine when young, Riesling is a much better wine with some bottle age, though few Rieslings are stored long enough to show their best. Hillcrest Rieslings are given a better chance. Sommer does not release them until about two years after the vintage, fully ready to drink, though still receptive to longer aging.

Hillcrest's Rieslings are fermented at a temperature of 50 degrees in stainless steel tanks. At about two percent sugar, fermentation is stopped. In the best years, when the grapes have ripened exceptionally well, Sommer releases a late harvest Riesling which is more intense and usually slightly sweeter than his regular bottling. Sommer has also made Riesling ice wine. The grapes are picked frozen on the vine and quickly crushed before they thaw. The sweetest berries freeze the least, and in the first pressing, only the juice from the ripest berries is released. True ice wines are much more concentrated than their regularly picked brethren.

Best known for his Rieslings, Sommer has also made a mark with the small quantities of red wines he produces. All his red wines are aged in a combination of French and American oak. Pinot Noir has been successful, and in warmer years, Cabernet Sauvignon ripens well and is a wine for laying down. In 1974, Sommer set aside a Cabernet made from his oldest vines. A wine for long aging, Sommer did not release it for sale until eight years after the vintage.

Richard Sommer.

Zinfandel, a long season grape, seldom ripens properly in Oregon, but in choice years, when the grape does ripen, the wine can be very good. Hillcrest, in very small quantities, is one of the few Northwest wineries producing a Zinfandel, and in those rare good years, it is a most worthy wine.

The trip from Roseburg to the Hillcrest winery is rather convoluted, entailing a number of turns and side roads, but the route is well marked with winery signs, and once there, the visitor is offered a wide selection of wines from different grapes and different vintages for tasting and purchase. Hillcrest wines are available throughout western Oregon, but may soon become more widely distributed. Some of Hillcrest's speciality wines are for sale only at the winery.

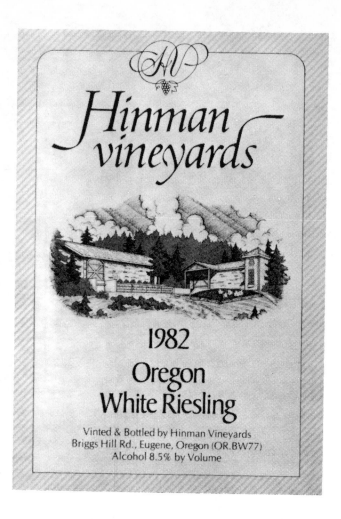

Hinman
vineyards

1982
Oregon
White Riesling

Vinted & Bottled by Hinman Vineyards
Briggs Hill Rd., Eugene, Oregon (OR.BW77)
Alcohol 8.5% by Volume

Hinman Vineyards

Founded 1979
27012 Briggs Hill Road, Eugene, Oregon 97405
(503) 345-1945

Saturday and Sunday, Noon to 5 PM.

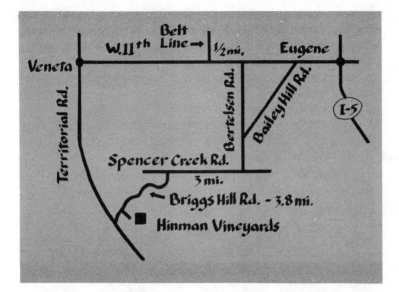

HINMAN VINEYARDS

The Oregon wine industry, now two decades old, has taken on some semblance of stability. Pinot Noir, Chardonnay, and Riesling are the three principal varieties. Winemaking methods vary, but are generally similar. The industry, however, is far from stagnant. Interest continues in other growing sites, other varieties, and alternate styles of making wine.

Hinman Vineyards, a partnership of Doyle Hinman and David Smith, varies from the established norm more than most. Doyle Hinman has worked and studied at the Geisenheim Institute in Germany. While Oregon winegrowers look primarily to France's Burgundy district for perspective on their own winemaking methods and styles, Hinman's Geisenheim experience has significantly influenced his own winemaking approach.

Among its activities, the Geisenheim Institute develops new vinifera grape crosses for Germany's cool winegrowing climates. During his study, Hinman helped make the wine from the experimental grape varieties. German wines, whether experimental or not, can be generally characterized as flavorful but delicate, low in alcohol, and fairly high in acid. The white wines are almost always

81

Doyle Hinman and David Smith.

made with some residual sugar, which in combination with the higher acidity, gives German wines their characteristic piquancy.

Hinman's Riesling and Gewurztraminer, like most produced in Oregon, are made in the Germanic style. A wine with residual sugar can be made either by stopping fermentation before all the sugar has fermented, or by fermenting the wine to dryness, then adding unfermented grape juice to the wine. This latter practice, called the "sweet reserve" method is prevalent in Germany, and it is the method Hinman uses for his wines.

Hinman's Chardonnay is unconventional. Most Oregon Chardonnay is fermented to dryness, put through a "secondary" malolactic fermentation to reduce its acidity, and aged in oak barrels. Hinman's Chardonnay is not put through a malolactic fermentation. It is fermented and aged in stainless steel, and finished with a slight amount of residual sugar. Occasionally, the Chardonnay is blended with Sauvignon Blanc, a once underrated but now increasingly popular grape variety.

Although most Hinman white wines are finished with some residual sugar, few could be called sweet. The residual sugar is minimal, just enough to balance the acidity and engender the stylistic piquancy.

The red wines, Cabernet Sauvignon from southern Oregon, and Pinot Noir, are made in traditional styles. Some Pinot Noir, however, does go into the production of Hinman's popular White Pinot Noir.

Hinman's devotion to Germanic wine styles is not confined only to winemaking methods. Hinman has planted small plots of Limberger and Ehrenfelser, two German grape varieties uncommon to Oregon. Limberger is grown principally in Germany's Wurttemberg region where it produces delicate, fruity, red wines. Ehrenfelser, a grape developed at the Geisenheim Institute, is one of the most successful crosses of Riesling and Sylvaner. The variety ripens earlier than Riesling, and the quality of the fruit is excellent. If the grapes from the experimental plots are successful, more acreage will be planted to them.

Hinman's vineyard consists of ten acres. Smith's nearby vineyard is nine acres, but he has purchased an additional 54 acres, much of which is suitable for grape growing. Hinman is also looking to buy more vineyard land in the area. Both Smith and Hinman regard their small valley as a distinctive microclimate, and are hoping that the area will eventually have its own officially recognized appellation.

Hinman Vineyards produces 15,000 gallons annually, but the winery can accommodate a yearly production of 60,000 gallons, and expansion is planned. The winery is not just a production facility. The grounds and buildings have been very attractively designed with visitors in mind. Picnicking on the grounds is encouraged, and during the summer months, jazz and classical music festivals are held in an outdoor amphitheater.

Knudsen Erath Winery
Founded 1967
Route 1, Box 368, Dundee, Oregon 97115
(503) 538-3318

Saturday and Sunday, Noon to 5 PM; Monday through Friday, 10 AM to 3 PM.

Second tasting room:
691 Highway 99 West, Dundee, Oregon 97115.

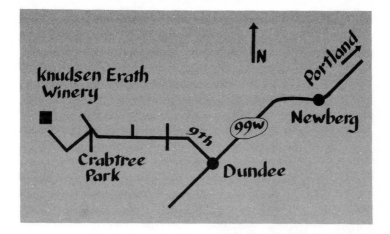

KNUDSEN ERATH WINERY

Dick Erath is another of the genuine pioneers of the Oregon wine industry, one of the early few who came to Oregon in the 1960's to make wine. A home winegrower and electronics engineer from California, Erath became interested in starting a commercial winery. On a trip through Oregon in 1967, Erath bought some grapes and made them into wine. Impressed with the quality, Erath and his family purchased vineyard acreage in the Chehalem foothills in Oregon's northern Willamette Valley, and moved from California to start their new winery.

Later, in 1972, Erath developed a vineyard for Cal Knudsen in the Red Hills, near Dundee, Oregon. Erath and Knudsen wanted to have their own separate wineries, but share the cost and use of expensive winemaking equipment. Legal restrictions prevented them from carrying out their plans, and, instead, the two men joined in partnership in 1975 and formed the Knudsen Erath Winery. For a time, the wines were sold under separate as well as joint labels, but beginning in 1979, Knudsen Erath adopted a single uniform label for all their wines.

Knudsen Erath is Oregon's largest winery, producing more than 80,000 gallons of wine a year. The winery, tasting room, and Knudsen's 70 acre vineyard are just a few miles outside the town of Dundee. Erath's 30 acre vineyard is located five miles north of the winery. Within a few years, Knudsen Erath expects to have 125 vineyard acres, purchase additional grapes from other Oregon growers, and produce up to 100,000 gallons of wine a year.

Regional tastes differ. Curiously, some of Oregon's finer wines are appreciated more on the east coast than in the Northwest. Riesling and Chardonnay, both very good wines for that matter, are most popular in Oregon. Pinot Noir, the state's unquestioned star, is not yet as well appreciated by the average Oregon consumer. While east coast palates are more familiar with red Burgundies and European wines in general, tastes more akin to Oregon wines than California wines, Northwest palates have been steeped in the organoleptic mind set of California wine. Good Pinot Noir is more scarce than good Chardonnay, and in the east coast markets, Erath reports sales of two bottles of his Pinot Noir for every one of Chardonnay. Compared to the prices of French Burgundies, Erath notes, Oregon Pinot Noirs are outstanding values.

Pinot Noir is Knudsen Erath's best wine. In the late 60's, when Riesling was still the "safe" grape to grow in this new and uncertain winegrowing region, Dick Erath was one of the early pioneers giving significant emphasis to Pinot Noir, and in the early and mid 70's, when Oregon Pinot Noir was not yet consistently good, Erath developed a reputation for producing some of the best.

Knudsen Erath's Pinot Noir is primarily the Pommard clone. Erath believes that Pommard may offer a bit more on the palate than other clones, though perhaps with less nose than the Wadenswil clone, but he emphasizes that microclimate, viticultural and winemaking practices, and year to year variation have far more effect than any clonal differences. Erath excepts the Gamay clone from this view. The Gamay has bigger berries and clusters and a higher acid to sugar ratio. Erath does not care for Gamay, and blends the little he has into a generic red.

Oregon State University is one of the three sites in the United States authorized to "import" grape vines. Through OSU, Knudsen Erath has obtained and planted experimental plots of 13 different Pinot Noir clones from around the world. Besides potential taste differences, clones have different growing patterns and ripening characteristics. Experimentation with clones may help fine tune winegrowing practices.

Erath ferments his Pinot Noir in closed, 2,000 gallon stainless steel tanks, and macerates the rising cap of skins and pulp by pumping the must over and through it under high pressure. Erath believes that the closed tank keeps the volatile flavor constituents

Dick Erath

from escaping, condensing them back into the must. Erath in-
oculates the must to undergo malolactic fermentation concurrently with the alcohol fermentation. It has been Erath's experience that
the troublesome haze sometimes associated with malolactic fermentation is not present when the fermentations are run concurrently.
A further advantage is that the winemaker does not have to delay
adding sulfur dioxide while waiting for the bacterial malolactic
fermentation, thereby insuring more immediate stability against
contamination.

Erath explains how the vines are hedged between the rows to remove excess foliage.

Erath allows the must to reach 86 degrees, and at the height of fermentation, pumps the must over the cap every two hours. Fermentation is usually completed in five days. At seven days, the wine cools to about 65 degrees, the cap is nearly sunk, malolactic fermentation is complete, and the wine is pressed and racked into French oak where it ages for 11 months. Twenty percent of the barrels are renewed each year.

In 1980, for the first time in nine vintages, Erath chaptalized Pinot Noir. Part was moderately chaptalized to raise the sugar content of the grape must from 21½ degrees Brix to 22½ degrees Brix. The remainder was left unchaptalized. Erath was quite pleased with the character of the chaptalized wine, and in the future, if the harvest should again dictate, Erath will moderately chaptalize all the must.

Chardonnay, Riesling, and Pinot Noir are Knudsen Erath's major wines. Smaller quantities of other varieties are also produced, including, in some years, an excellent Oregon Sauvignon Blanc. The best wines from the best years are given the designation "Vintage Select."

Sparkling wine is a new and major trend in Oregon winemaking. Erath's early experiments with small lots of sparkling wine gave way to a full scale commercial commitment to the wine. New vineyards have been planted on cooler slopes for a steady supply of suitable grapes, and in cooler vintages, Erath sets aside less ripe grapes for the sparkling wine. To make premium sparkling wine, still wine is put in "tirage," into bottles along with sugar and yeast to ferment again slightly, creating the wine's sparkle and special flavors. A thousand cases of a Pinot Noir and Chardonnay cuvee went into tirage in October of 1982.

MULHAUSEN

1982

Willamette Valley

White Riesling

VINEYARDS

A medium dry white wine with a distinguishable varietal character
Vinted and Bottled by Chehalem Mountain Winery
Newberg, Ore. B. W. O. R.78
Alc 10½ % by Vol.

Mulhausen Vineyards
(Chehalem Mountain Winery)
Founded 1979
Route 1, Box 99C, Newberg, Oregon 97132
(503) 628-2417

Weekends and holidays, Noon to 5 PM.

90

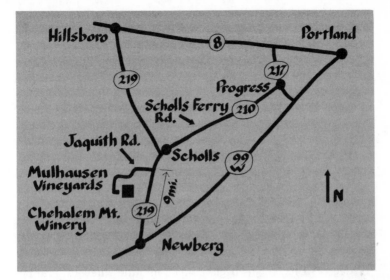

MULHAUSEN VINEYARDS

Zane Mulhausen developed an interest in wine while in Europe in the 1950's. Returning to his native Oregon, he held in his mind the idea that the Willamette Valley ought to be a good place to grow grapes and make fine wines. In 1969, Mulhausen purchased land that would become his vineyard site. In 1973, he planted grapes, and in 1979, the winery was bonded under the name Chehalem Mountain Winery. The wines are released under the name Mulhausen Vineyards.

A mechanical engineer by profession, Mulhausen turned to work in the construction industry in the boom years of the 1970's. In 1980, he retired to work full time in the vineyard and winery. Twenty acres are planted. Forty-five more will be added at the rate of about ten a year. Mulhausen is winemaker. David Wirtz, formerly of the now defunct Reuter's Hill winery, is consultant.

The soil is a deep Chehalem Mountain Jory, running eighty feet to rock. Six inches down, the soil is red. It is a shot soil, containing hard, relatively insoluble nodules of clay the size of a B-B, making the soil more permeable and providing good drainage.

Typically, Oregon vineyards are planted on the southernmost sides of mountain ranges on slopes with southern, preferably southeastern, exposures. Somewhat unusually, the Mulhausen vineyard is planted on the northern side of the Chehalem Mountains, though on a slope with nearly the ideal southeastern exposure. Southeastern exposures catch the first rays of morning sun to warm and dry the vineyard from the cool night. Mulhausen reports that his grapes ripen at about the same time with about the same sugar and acid levels as other Willamette Valley vineyards.

As with most Oregon growers, Mulhausen is plagued with robins. The local robins are less offensive, learning more readily about shotguns and noise cannons. The massive Canadian migrations, however, present a continuing problem as wave after wave move through the Willamette Valley. Mulhausen reports that robins provide a good indication of grape ripening. Before sugar levels reach 17 degrees Brix, robins show little interest in the grapes. At 17 degrees Brix, robins begin coming into the vineyard, and by 18 degrees Brix, their interest is intense. A pair of Mulhausen's hunting dogs work the vineyard rows, helping to frighten the robins. As the vineyard's size increases, Mulhausen will turn to netting to protect the grapes. At harvest, the grapes are picked into five gallon buckets, then dumped into 1,000 pound totes.

Only French oak is used to age Mulhausen's wines. In Oregon, it is frequent practice to ferment as well as age Chardonnay in small oak barrels, but believing that fermenting in stainless steel better insures cleanliness, Mulhausen shuns oak for fermentation in favor of stainless steel tanks and barrels, fermentation containers that are also more suited to his preference for preserving in the wine more of the fruity quality of the grape. Fermenting white wines at cooler temperatures also emphasizes this quality. Mulhausen's first wines were fermented with Montrachet yeast, but Montrachet is not the best performing strain at lower temperatures, and having had problems with fermentations that were reluctant to carry through to completion, Mulhausen now uses Champagne and Steinberg strains.

Mulhausen buys Sylvaner grapes from a Washington County grower, and produces the only varietally labeled release of this wine in Oregon. An unusual wine, Sylvaner is both Riesling-like and earthy. Like Gewurztraminer, it is not for everyone's taste, but those who enjoy the wine can find it nowhere else in Oregon. Supply is limited, and Mulhausen will probably plant some vines of his own to satisfy the demand.

Zane Mulhausen.

Besides Sylvaner, Mulhausen produces Riesling, Chardonnay, Pinot Noir, and Gewurztraminer. In his own vineyard, Pinot Noir is planted half to the Wadenswil clone and half to Pommard in alternate rows. In cooler years, a sparkling wine will be made from a cuvee of Chardonnay and Pinot Noir.

The tasting room, run by Zane's wife Pat, is in a converted portion of the Mulhausens' large and massively constructed home. Designed and built by Mulhausen from four kinds of custom cut wood, the structure makes modern "spec homes" seem utterly fragile in comparison. The tasting room feels as if it is still an integral part of the home, and is adjoined by a comfortable sitting area with a picture window view. Wines for tasting are served on an antique seventeenth century table.

VINTAGE 1982
OREGON WHITE RIESLING

A dry white wine with a fragrant aroma and rich, fruity flavor

OREGON BONDED WINERY NO. 50
PRODUCED & BOTTLED BY OAK KNOLL WINERY, INC., HILLSBORO, OR

ALCOHOL 12½% BY VOLUME

Oak Knoll Winery
Founded 1970
Route 6, Box 184, Burkhalter Road, Hillsboro, Oregon 97123
(503) 648-8198

Thursday, Friday, and Sunday, 1 PM to 5 PM; Saturday, 11 AM to 5 PM; other days by appointment.

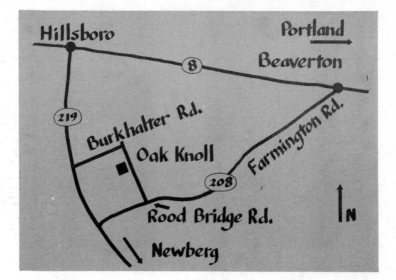

OAK KNOLL WINERY

Each year, on the third weekend in May, Oak Knoll hosts the "Bacchus Goes Bluegrass Wine Festival," an event that draws nearly 20,000 visitors to the rural setting that was once the site of a dairy farm. Ron and Marjorie Vuylsteke, the principal owners and operators of Oak Knoll, have seen their winery grow from one gallon of homemade blackberry wine to an annual production of 50,000 gallons.

Interest in home winemaking lead to the founding of Oak Knoll Winery in 1970, and a first year production of 4,000 gallons. By 1978, a third of all Oregon wine sold within the state was produced by Oak Knoll. Although the accelerated growth of the Oregon wine industry has caused Oak Knoll's percentage of the marketplace to decrease, Oak Knoll remains one of Oregon's larger wineries.

Oak Knoll began as a fruit and berry winery, and continues primarily as such, but of the 50,000 gallons produced each year, 20,000 are made from vinifera grapes, and vinifera wines are playing an increasingly important role at Oak Knoll. The old dairy barn

The wines.

that in 1970 seemed much too large for their winery, became much too small, and a second building was built to house the tasting room, office, and bottling and storage facilities.

The Vuylstekes own no vinifera vineyards of their own, and must rely on private growers for their grapes. This arrangement offers less control over the grapes, and less assurance of continuity from year to year, but there are also some advantages. Less capital is tied up in land and vines, more grapes can be purchased in better years and fewer in less favorable years, and the winery is not tied to a single growing area and a fixed number of grape varieties, but is free to explore new varieties and growing areas as they evolve.

Some of the winemaking philosophies developed with the fruit and berry wines are carried over to grape winemaking. The Vuylstekes believe that preservation of the fruity qualities inherent in the grape is an important consideration in making grape wines.

Red wines are traditionally fermented in open top containers, but the Vuylstekes cover their redwood tanks with plastic tarps to trap volatile flavor constituents that would normally escape into the air, and condense them back into the wine. The use of older oak barrels for aging also emphasizes more of the fruit of the grape rather than the flavor of the oak.

Contrary to traditional practice, Oak Knoll's first red wines were not put through a malolactic fermentation, a procedure that yields rounder, more complex wines, though at the expense of some of the flavors of the grape. But in 1979, Oak Knoll purchased French oak barrels that originally came from Chateau Lafite-Rothschild. These barrels retained the malolactic organism, and now Oak Knoll's red wines automatically go through a malolactic fermentation.

After crushing and prior to fermentation, the white wine must is kept in contact with the skins at least overnight. After fermentation is completed, the wines are centrifuged and pumped into barrels or tanks. At one time, the red wines were also centrifuged, but it was found that some of the flavoring constituents were stripped away, and the practice was discontinued.

Oak Knoll's wines are by no means outside of the mainstream of winemaking styles and tastes, but they do carry the signature of an individual's winemaking philosophy. Vuylsteke has assisted some of the Northwest's more promising new wineries in their first years of production, providing encouragement and technical assistance to Idaho's Facelli Vineyards and Oregon's Shafer Vineyard Cellars.

Oak Knoll's fruit and berry wines are exceptionally good, and vinifera winedrinkers should not totally dismiss them out of hand. Gooseberry and rhubarb will probably find most favor for those with a vinifera palate, although some of the other berry wines offer a fresh taste and change of pace.

Oak Knoll has opened a second tasting room, Shipwreck Cellars, in Lincoln City, Oregon, overlooking the Pacific Ocean. The address is 3521 S.W. Highway 101. Shipwreck Cellars is open daily from 10 AM to 6 PM.

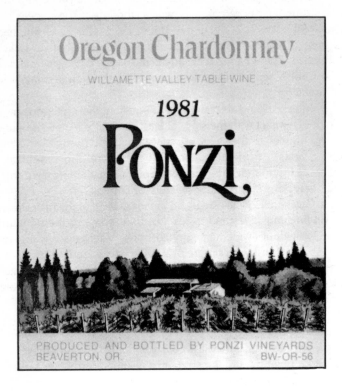

Oregon Chardonnay

WILLAMETTE VALLEY TABLE WINE

1981

PONZI

PRODUCED AND BOTTLED BY PONZI VINEYARDS
BEAVERTON, OR.   BW-OR-56

Ponzi Vineyards
Founded 1970
Route 1, Box 842, Beaverton, Oregon 97005
(503) 628-1227

Saturday and Sunday, Noon to 5 PM.
Closed January and holidays.

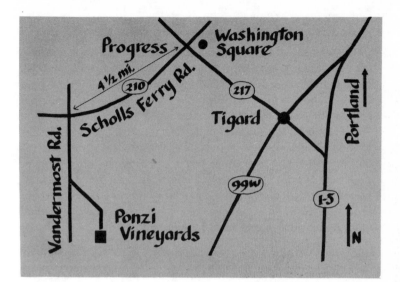

PONZI VINEYARDS

Ponzi Vineyards, located 15 miles from Portland and only a few miles from a large shopping center, is nevertheless very much in a rural setting. If approached by back roads, there would be little indication of Ponzi's proximity to the urban milieu. Residents have battled back the urban sprawl, and favorable zoning has prohibited further subdivision in the area.

The vineyard's microclimate and soil are different from others in the Willamette Valley. Though most vineyards are planted up to a 1,000 feet above sea level on sloping hillsides, the Ponzi vineyard is planted in sandy benchland at an elevation of 250 feet. Nearby soil is quite claylike. Ponzi's sandier soil may be attributable to geologic changes in the course of the nearby Tualatin River. Although the vineyard has a slight southerly slope, the land is generally level. Concerns that insufficient air drainage would cause frost problems proved unfounded. Air movement has been more than adequate, flowing through the vineyard and dropping over the bench into the valley.

The Ponzi family owns the 17 acre estate and makes their home on the property. Ten acres are planted to grapes. Ten thousand gallons of wine are produced each year. Additional grapes are purchased on long-term contract from two other vineyards, Five Mountain Vineyard near Hillsboro and Medici Vineyard near Newberg, both within ten miles of the winery, yet producing grapes with subtle qualitative differences.

Opposed to pesticide and herbicide spraying, the Ponzis have found that ladybugs and other beneficial insects are attracted to the vineyards, helping to maintain balance in its ecosystem. Also emphatically opposed to Mesurol, a chemical spray that deters birds by making them ill, the Ponzis net their vineyards as harvest approaches. Costly and time consuming, netting is an effective method of protecting the grapes from hungry birds.

Chardonnay, Pinot Noir, and Riesling are the major varieties grown in the Ponzi vineyard. In 1981, Pinot Gris, a now rare variety that promises to become one of Oregon's major wine grapes, was added to Ponzi's repertoire of wines. In 1982, Ponzi side-grafted two acres of Pinot Blanc and Gewurztraminer over to Pinot Gris, and planted an additional acre of the variety.

The Pinot Noir planting consists of two clones—Pommard, and a clone obtained from California's Mirassou winery. Ponzi reports differences in their growing characteristics. The Mirassou clone is easier to train and produces a darker wine, but also ripens later than the Pommard clone, a characteristic that can cause problems in less favorable vintages.

Ponzi's Pinot Noir is fermented in small open containers. At first, Ponzi limited fermentation temperatures to 70 degrees or lower, but temperatures are now allowed to reach 80 degrees for better character and color extraction. After fermentation, the Pinot Noir is put into French oak barrels to age. Except for a light egg white fining in some vintages, the wine is neither fined nor filtered.

Ponzi, an advocate of oak barrel fermentation for Chardonnay, prefers Allier oak to Limousin. Limousin, he feels, gives a less desirable lemon flavor to the wine. Comparing his own experiences, Ponzi indicates that oak fermented wines begin malolactic fermentation more easily and continue it more smoothly and consistently. The wines clear more rapidly, and although they do not necessarily have a stronger oak taste, they display a rounder fuller character. Ponzi ferments his Chardonnay at very cool temperatures, and the wine may require as much as two months for the fermentation to finish.

Richard Ponzi.

The Riesling is made in a dry style, and finished without wood aging. Fermented at about 50 degrees, the wine sometimes requires up to four months to complete fermentation. Particularly with Riesling, most winemakers feel a cool fermentation produces a fresher wine and preserves more of the delicate flavors of the grape.

The Ponzi winery is built of stone from a nearby quarry. Its roof is made of an expensive, highly durable material designed to oxidize with exposure to the elements, forming a protective barrier, and an attractive patina that changes color with the weather. The comfortable tasting room is available for private receptions and meetings, and the spacious lawn provides a setting for larger gatherings and festivals. Ponzi maintains a mailing list for announcement of new releases and special events.

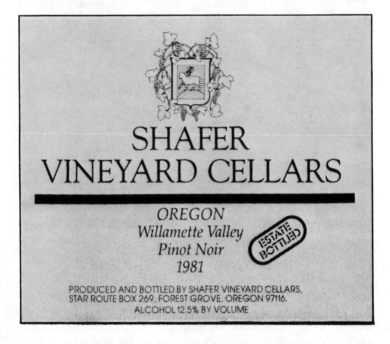

SHAFER
VINEYARD CELLARS

OREGON
Willamette Valley
Pinot Noir
1981

ESTATE BOTTLED

PRODUCED AND BOTTLED BY SHAFER VINEYARD CELLARS,
STAR ROUTE BOX 269, FOREST GROVE, OREGON 97116.
ALCOHOL 12.5% BY VOLUME

Shafer Vineyard Cellars

Founded 1981
Star Route, Box 269, Forest Grove, Oregon 97116
(503) 357-6604

Weekends and most holidays, Noon to 5 PM. Closed January.

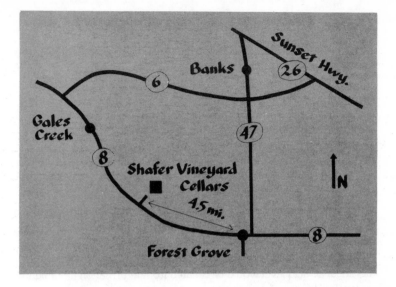

SHAFER VINEYARD CELLARS

Harvey and Linda Shafer wanted only to be grape growers. Fortunately, their original intent was not fulfilled, and Shafer Vineyard Cellars has become one of Oregon's finest newer wineries. The vineyards were planted in 1973. For a time, Shafer supplied other Oregon wineries with grapes, but as Linda Shafer says, "Just being growers was like being pregnant for five years and giving away the baby," so the the Shafer's decided to start a winery.

Because of long delays in building the winery, the 1978 vintage was made at Elk Cove, and the 1979 and 1980 vintages were made at Oak Knoll. These three vintages not only provided winemaking instruction for Harvey Shafer, but allowed him to begin implementing his own stylistic preferences. The wines from these years were well crafted. The winery was finally completed in the summer of 1981, and that fall, Shafer vinified his first crush. 1981 was a cool and rainy vintage, a difficult year for both the grower and winemaker. Shafer believes that 80% of a wine's quality comes from the vineyard. With his first crush, Shafer demonstrated that he also does well with the other 20%.

Nearly all the grapes for Shafer's wines come from the Shafer estate. The 20 acre vineyard, in the narrow Gales Creek Valley, is at an average elevation of 450 feet. An additional ten more acres will be planted.

Shafer's talk of microclimates and vineyard interrelationships brings home the importance of grape growing to winemaking. Across the narrow valley, the exposures are more northerly and the hillsides are often shrouded in fog. Even sites with southern exposures on the "good side" of the Gales Creek and Tualatin River Valleys can vary markedly. Vineyards within six miles of each other ripen as much as three weeks apart. A winemaker must have a close relationship with the vineyards. Citing an example of this, Shafer points out that grapes become "ripe" at different sugar levels, depending on the vintage and vineyard site. Shafer not only measures the grape sugar as harvest approaches, but also tastes the grapes. A winemaker instructing a grower only to pick at a certain sugar or acid level would be isolated from information that might make the difference between a merely good wine and a wine of excellence.

Some Oregon wineries emphasize the delicate fruit flavors of the grape. Others prefer a style that emphasizes the transformation of these ethereal flavors and scents into more rounded, fuller flavors with less fruit of the grape, but perhaps more complex character. Although such dichotomies are inevitably oversimplified, Shafer largely falls into the latter category.

The difference in style can be observed in the making of their Chardonnay. Shafer ferments the Chardonnay in oak barrels rather than stainless steel and uses the Montrachet yeast strain which has a reputation for extracting fuller flavors, but at the risk of an undesireable hydrogen sulfide byproduct. To guard against hydrogen sulfide, Shafer applies no sulphur after July, and racks the wine (removes it from the remaining grape solids) immediately after fermentation is complete. Shafer Chardonnays display the positive aspects of Montrachet yeast without its undesireable byproducts. The wine is aged in Limousin and Never oak barrels.

Shafer is rapidly achieving a reputation for its Pinot Noir. Instead of fermenting in the more convenient stainless steel tanks, Shafer, like many Oregon wineries, ferments in bins four feet square and two feet deep. Lined with food grade plastic, the maraschino cherry brining bins are ideal fermentation containers. As Pinot Noir ferments, the skins and pulp rises to form a cap. In tanks, wine is pumped over the cap to resubmerge it. In the bins, the cap is

Linda and Harvey Shafer.

punched down, squeezed, and macerated by the physical action, a process thought by some to be superior for extracting flavors from the grape. Shafer's Pinot Noir is then aged in Allier oak barrels.

In addition to Pinot Noir, Riesling, and Chardonnay, the Shafer's produce small quantities of Sauvignon Blanc. According to viticultural texts, the grape ripens late, and thus would not be ideally suited to the Willamette Valley climate. In Shafer's experience, however, the grape ripens as early as Pinot Noir. In cool years, like other varieties, it suffers from lack of ripeness, but unlike some varieties, varietal flavors begin to show early. The grape, particularly at lower levels of ripeness, has a pronounced grassy character that is not to everyone's taste, but it has long been an underrated variety that has just recently seen increased popularity. Little is planted in Oregon, but the Shafer's have helped demonstrate the grape's potential.

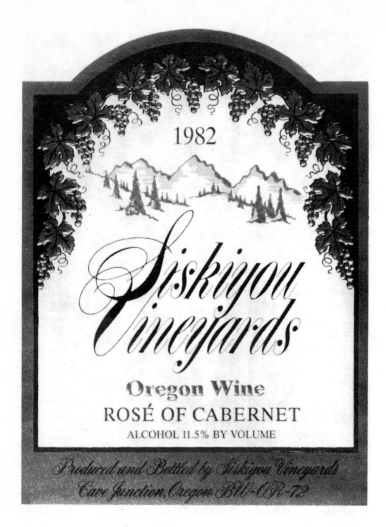

1982

*Siskiyou
Vineyards*

Oregon Wine
ROSÉ OF CABERNET
ALCOHOL 11.5% BY VOLUME

*Produced and Bottled by Siskiyou Vineyards
Cave Junction, Oregon BW-OR-72*

Siskiyou Vineyards
Founded 1978
6220 Caves Highway, Cave Junction, Oregon 97523
(503) 592-3727

Daily, 11 AM to 4 PM.

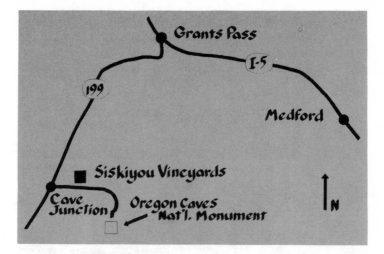

SISKIYOU VINEYARDS

Located in the Illinois Valley of southernmost Oregon, not far from the California border, Siskiyou Vineyards is in a climate quite different from northern Oregon's Willamette Valley, or even the Umpqua Valley near Roseburg in the southerly portion of the state. Siskiyou's owner, Suzi David, is the first in the modern era to establish an Illinois Valley winery. The climate is quite warm compared to the other growing areas of western Oregon, although not quite as warm as the nearby Applegate Valley to the east, the site of southern Oregon's only other major winery.

At 1,200 feet above sea level, Siskiyou is slightly higher than most other Oregon vineyards. Because summers are warm, and the soil, a Josephine loam, runs only three to five feet deep, holding little water, irrigation is a necessity. Spring frosts can be a problem, and overhead sprinkler systems not only provide irrigation for the vineyards during summer, but also protection against the frosts.

There are remnants of pre-prohibition vines here and there in the Illinois Valley, but the area lay viticulturally stagnant until Charles Coury of the now defunct Charles Coury winery in the northern Willamette Valley came to Rogue Community College in 1972, and taught a course on enology and viticulture. As a result

Suzi David.

of the course, a number of area residents got cuttings from Coury and later planted vineyards. Most of the first plantings were modest, a few vines for a hobby, but the outcome was predictable and in- evitable. The previous owner of David's property had been one of those who had attended the lectures and planted a few vines. After acquiring the property, David planted a full-fledged vineyard. Twelve acres are now bearing, and fifteen more will soon be put to vine.

In 1981, Siskiyou produced 3,500 gallons, in 1982, 12,000, and in a few years, a production of 15,000 to 25,000 gallons is expected. Siskiyou's grapes come from several growing areas in southern Oregon, but eventually, as David's own vineyards and others in the valley mature, all Siskiyou's wines will be made from grapes grown in the Illinois Valley.

Siskiyou produces Cabernet Sauvignon, Merlot, Pinot Noir, Zinfandel, Semillon, Riesling, Sauvignon Blanc, Chenin Blanc, Chardonnay, and Gewurztraminer. As in most of Oregon, Merlot suffers from very poor berry set in the spring, and thus small and unreliable crop yields, but one vineyard near Medford has had con- sistently good berry set, and Siskiyou, among others, will be bud- ding over some of their vines with this clone in hopes that Merlot will become commercially viable.

In the Illinois Valley, growing conditions vary considerably from vintage to vintage, but generally, grape ripening is about two weeks ahead of the Roseburg area, and Cabernet Sauvignon does especially well.

Siskiyou's first wines were made in a tiny, cramped, winery area, and there was not enough room to age any of the wines in oak, but beginning in 1981, all the red wines were aged in Limousin oak barrels, and in 1982, a large, modern facility was constructed with ample room for oak barrels and temperature controlled fermentation tanks.

Located on the highway to the famous Oregon Caves National Monument, the Siskiyou winery offers an attractive side stop for visitors. The new tasting room is finished in redwood, and features the work of local artists. In the spring, an art, music, and wine festival is held on Siskiyou's two acre trout lake.

SB

Sokol Blosser

1981

Yamhill County
Chardonnay

A crisp, fragrant chardonnay, aged gently in Limousin Oak, produced from grapes grown in Yamhill County, in the Willamette Valley of Oregon.

PRODUCED AND BOTTLED BY
SOKOL BLOSSER WINERY, DUNDEE, OREGON (BW-OR-66)
Alcohol 13.5% by Volume

Sokol Blosser Winery
Founded 1977
P.O. Box 199, Blanchard Lane, Dundee, Oregon 97115
(503) 864-3342

Daily, Noon to 5 PM.

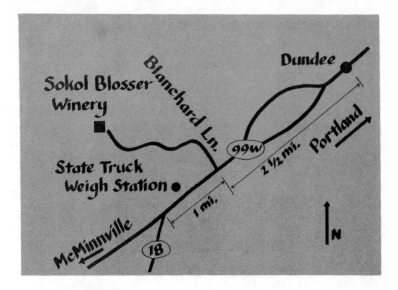

SOKOL BLOSSER WINERY

Family owned, Sokol Blosser is one of Oregon's three largest wineries, producing 65,000 gallons of wine a year. The winery building and facilities are at capacity, and Sokol Blosser is poised for major expansion whenever financial and market conditions dictate.

Size is relative, and in some contexts Sokol Blosser would be considered quite small, but in Oregon, wineries traditionally have begun with a few acres of vines, and a garage, basement, or shed to serve as a winery. Sokol Blosser was among the first to start with a modern, well-financed operation.

The winery's size was dictated by personal preferences and interrelated economic necessities. In 1971, Bill and Susan Blosser planted 18 acres of grapes. In 1974, the vines began to bear fruit and the grapes were sold to neighboring wineries. The Blossers had decided that they would not build a winery until they were certain it would be economically viable. Studies were made. Not wanting to rely on their own winemaking skills, the Blossers decided that a full-time winemaker would be needed. The salary for a pro-

The Sokol Blosser tasting room.

fessional winemaker, as well as other considerations, indicated that a fairly large winery was necessary for cost efficiency.

In 1977, financing was obtained through the formation of a limited partnership consisting of Bill Blosser and Susan Sokol Blosser as general partners, and members of Susan Blosser's family as limited partners. Bob McRitchie, then chief chemist for Franciscan Vineyards, was hired as winemaker. A 6,400 square foot facility was built, and the 1977 crush was on.

The winery building, built of prestressed concrete, is set into a rocky knoll. Adjacent to the winery is the tasting room, an attractive modern structure designed by the noted architect, John Storrs. In addition to wines for tasting and purchase, the tasting room also has for sale wine-related items and fruit and nuts from the Sokol Blosser orchards. During harvest, a bowl of wine grapes is set out for sampling. Undoubtedly Oregon's most popular winery for touring, each year 20,000 visitors pass through Sokol Blosser's tasting room. Equipped with a kitchen, the tasting room is available for dinners and receptions.

Sokol Blosser has 45 acres planted to vine and 30 more acres available for expansion. Eighty percent of production comes from purchased grapes. Initially, one third of the production came from Washington grapes, but now that the Oregon grape harvest has increased, fewer grapes are purchased from Washington. Sokol

Blosser's largest supplier is Hyland Vineyards, a 65 acre vineyard about 15 miles southwest of the winery near the town of Bellevue.

The American taste in recent years has run toward white wines. In certain respects, this trend has aided new wineries. Most white wines require less handling than red wines and can be released much sooner, tying up less capital and providing much needed cash flow to keep investors and bankers happy. Seventy percent of Sokol Blosser's production is in white wines, and the winery is working toward a goal of 80 percent. Sokol-Blosser was the first commercial producer of Muller-Thurgau in America. A Riesling-like grape, Muller-Thurgau is widely grown in Germany.

Of the whites, Chardonnay is Sokol Blosser's stellar wine. Popular taste runs toward lower acid wines, and indeed, when such wines are consumed alone, these types of wines have a certain appeal, but when consumed with food, as most wine is meant to be, lower acid wines become dull and cloying as the meal progresses, failing to cleanse and refresh the palate. Oregon wines are inherently higher in acid, but there is a tendency to release wines at lower acid levels to satisfy popular taste. Sokol Blosser's Chardonnay bucks this trend. Typically, the wine is tightly structured, and has sufficient acid to age well and marry well with food.

Whether in Oregon, California, or Burgundy, Pinot Noir is always a difficult grape. Pinot Noir is subject to wide clonal variation, different clones sometimes producing wines of considerably different character. Clonal selection is a continuing and no doubt unending debate. Sokol Blosser is participating in an experimental program of vine and grape evaluation. The test vines are planted near the winery's tasting room. A number of Pinot Noir clones have been planted, including some obtained directly from Europe. To date, results have been far from conclusive, and Bill Blosser believes that too much has been made of the importance of clonal selection for Pinot Noir. Blosser points out that Pinot Noir vines continually mutate throughout their existence, and that Burgundians do not try to maintain a single clone in their vineyards, but rather, when it is time to replant, replace old vines with about the same ratio of variations already present in the vineyard.

Another subject of debate concerns the effect of the soil on the taste of the wine. Traditionally, soil composition has been considered a critical factor in wine character and quality. Many European texts are devoted to detailed explanations of this view. Another viewpoint holds that soil is important only in terms of

113

Bill Blosser tastes Pinot Noir grapes for ripeness as harvest approaches.

drainage, permeability, and other such mundane considerations, the taste of the wine not affected by the soil's character.

Sokol Blosser's soil is a volcanic clay loam known as Jory. Certainly distinctive in appearance, the red soil provides a colorful backdrop for the vineyard's lush green foliage. Some growers in the area say grapes from this soil produce more robust, fuller flavored wines than grapes from more delicate soils found elsewhere in the Willamette Valley. In spite of the temptation offered by their distinctive soil, the Blossers do not subscribe to this view, believing that soil character does not affect the taste of the wine.

Sokol Blosser is experimenting with several vine pruning and training methods. Cordon pruning, a method common to California, relies on permanent lateral arms (branches) to sprout new growth each spring. So far, yields seem to decrease when this method is used, and variations of Oregon's traditional cane pruning still perform best.

Sokol Blosser wines are available in thirty states. Small quantities have also been available in Australia, Mexico, England, and France.

114

Tualatin

ESTATE BOTTLED
1980
WILLAMETTE VALLEY
**Oregon
Chardonnay**

GROWN, PRODUCED AND BOTTLED BY
TUALATIN VINEYARDS, FOREST GROVE, OREGON
BW-OR-55   Alcohol 12.5% by volume

Tualatin Vineyards
Founded 1973
Route 1, Box 339, Forest Grove, Oregon 97116
(503) 357-5005

Saturday and Sunday, 1 PM to 5 PM; other times by appointment. Closed during January.

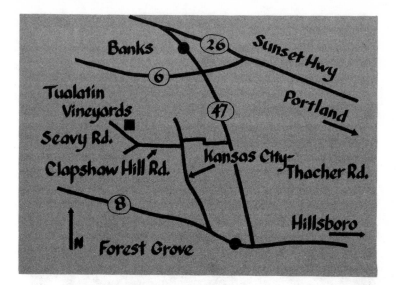

TUALATIN VINEYARDS

Discussions of wine frequently turn to talk of microclimates, the climatic differences among vineyards within a relatively small area that influence the character of the grapes and the wines made from them. Microclimate—the word trips glibly from the tongue, sometimes losing its meaning as if it were a mere abstraction not solidly connected with ongoing reality. It is, for this reason, quite striking when one chances across some of the "grass roots reality" behind the abstract phrase. Local residents remember, as schoolchildren, the picking season in nearby strawberry farms, and their envy of the children who picked for the Spengler farm. The Spengler strawberries always ripened before anybody else's, and the lucky children who picked for them were frequently let out of school early.

This warmer "microclimate" is now the Tualatin vineyard, and it is now grapes instead of strawberries that ripen earlier. Tualatin wines often do display a riper, fuller-bodied character than the wines from other area vineyards, and in cooler, rainier years, earlier ripening is a decided advantage.

117

Bill Fuller.

Although small by many standards, Tualatin is one of Oregon's larger wineries. The winery estate consists of 158 acres. Riesling, Pinot Noir, Chardonnay, and Gewurztraminer make up the bulk of the 80 acre vineyard. Roughly 50,000 gallons of wine are made each year.

Tualatin began in the early 1970's when Bill Fuller and Bill Malkmus completed their search for a viticultural region suited to cooler climate, earlier maturing varieties of vinifera grapes. Fuller and Malkmus have different but complementary backgrounds.

Malkmus is a graduate of Stanford University and Harvard Business School. Formerly an investment banker in San Francisco, Malkmus works out of Tualatin's California office and is in charge of business operations and marketing.

Fuller holds an M.S. in Enology from the University of California at Davis and has long been involved with the wine industry. From 1964 to 1973, he was chief chemist and wine production manager with California's Louis M. Martini winery. Fuller lives on the Tualatin estate with his wife, Virginia, and is in charge of winemaking and vineyard operations.

From his nine years at Louis M. Martini, Fuller brings to Oregon much of the style and philosophy of a large California

118

winery. Modern technology is regarded as basic to the winery operation. Jacketed stainless steel tanks and a centrifuge, once almost antithetical to the concept of Oregon wine, are standard equipment at Tualatin.

Instead of planting vineyards and waiting for them to bear fruit, Fuller broke with the unwritten rule, and immediately began making wine from Washington grapes. The practice was subsequently adopted by most other northern Willamette Valley winemakers, though it is now fading as Oregon grape production is better able to meet the needs of Oregon winemakers.

From the beginning, Tualatin has emphasized cooler climate, white wine grapes. Eighty percent of the vineyard is planted to white wine varieties, and more acreage is planted to Riesling than any other grape. In view of the white wine boom, Tualatin's wine selection has played well to consumer tastes.

Tualatin has more Gewurztraminer acreage than most Oregon wineries, and Fuller has experimented with other white varieties, including Early Muscat, a seldom planted varietal that seems to do quite well in Tualatin's vineyard. The Burgundian grape varieties, Chardonnay and Pinot Noir, have been less emphasized, but the most recent vineyard expansion was devoted entirely to these two grapes.

Fuller believes that Riesling and Pinot Noir are the Willamette Valley's most important varieties. The additional recent planting of Pinot Noir is an acknowledgment of this belief, and the inevitable cyclic shift of consumer demand back toward red wines.

Tualatin's vines are planted on their own rootstock, and drip irrigated when young to encourage more rapid maturity. Trained high for greater sun exposure, the foliage is cut back in late summer to expose the grapes to more sunlight, a practice differing from that of California where the foliage is used to shield the grapes from sunburn.

With availability in 21 states and press coverage facilitated by a California marketing base, Tualatin, although on a much smaller scale, is helping to do for Oregon what Chateau Ste. Michelle has done for Washington—put the state on the marketing map and stimulated widespread interest in the area. In just a few short years, the Oregon wine industry has grown to the extent that wine sales to markets outside the Northwest are critical to the health of the industry. Tualatin's early marketing efforts have helped set the stage for the new growth.

Valley View Vineyard
Founded 1978
1000 Applegate Road, Jacksonville, Oregon 97530
(503) 899-8468

Daily, 11 AM to 5 PM, April 15 to January 1; Saturday and Sunday, 1 PM to 5 PM, January 1 to April 15. For tours, please call ahead if possible.

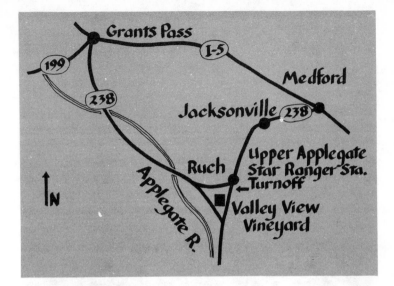

VALLEY VIEW VINEYARD

In 1972, the Wisnovsky family planted grapes in the Applegate Valley in southwest Oregon, marking the rediscovery of one of the Northwest's earliest viticultural regions. Western Oregon is known for its year-round temperate climate, richly foliaged landscapes, cloudy skies, and wet weather. Though this conception is substantially true for most of western Oregon, it does not apply to the climatic region centered in the Jacksonville area in the southwestern portion of the state, not far from California's border. This area is considerably sunnier, warmer, and drier than anywhere else in western Oregon. Grasses, long needle pines, and the absence of ubiquitous foliage demonstrate that this is indeed a much different climate.

Valley View is in the Applegate Valley at an elevation of 1,500 feet, in an area known as Sunshine Village. The soil in the 26 acre vineyard varies, but is predominantly a Ruch sandy loam. Most of the vineyard needs no irrigation, but in the shallower portions the soil is only 18 inches deep, and, in most years, these shallower areas need irrigation. Bud break occurs in mid-April. The

The Valley View Vineyard winery.

growing season is relatively short, and frost can be a problem in fall as well as spring.

John Eagle, once in the repertory company for Ashland's famous Oregon Shakespeare Festival, is Valley View's winemaker. Rob Stuart, a biochemistry graduate, is the assistant winemaker and vineyard manager.

Most areas in the Applegate Valley, including the Valley View vineyard site, are too warm for Gewurztraminer, Riesling, and Pinot Noir, so most of the grapes for these wines are purchased from vineyards in the cooler Illinois Valley to the west. In their own vineyards, Valley View is focusing on Cabernet Sauvignon and Chardonnay.

As in northern Oregon, Merlot does not set fruit well, and its yields are small and sporadic. At least one area grower, however, has had consistently good yields from the grape, and some think better clonal selection may be the key to better crops. Merlot ripens well, but is prone to dropping acidity quickly as ripeness approaches.

The Chardonnay is aged in air dried American oak, Cabernet and Merlot in French oak, and Pinot Noir in Yugoslavian oak.

Although kiln dried American oak barrels are cheaper than the air dried barrels, Eagle believes their flavors are too intrusive. Eagle likes the way Yugoslavian oak marries with Pinot Noir, imparting a pleasant cedar chest quality.

In this warmer growing area, the grapes are not as high in malic acid as those from northern Oregon, and malolactic fermentation, the conversion of malic acid to the less acidic lactic acid, is not as dramatic. Malolactic fermentation, however, does not merely lower the acidity of wine, it changes its character in a way that most feel is beneficial for most dry red and many dry white wines.

All of Valley View's oak aged wines go through malolactic fermentation. Malolactic bacteria, once it is present in the barrels, multiplies and becomes active again as the barrels are filled with new wine. The process, thus, occurs of its own accord, and the wine does not require inoculation from commercial cultures.

Valley view produces 12,000 gallons of wine a year. As the vineyard is brought into shape, production will grow to 20,000 gallons. Cabernet Sauvignon and Chardonnay have shown particular promise. Sauvignon Blanc has been very good, but Valley View has so little, it is blended into their white table wine. More Sauvignon Blanc may be planted. Valley View also produces Oregon Perry, a tasty fruit wine made from pears.

OTHER OREGON WINERIES

The
Red Hills
Vineyard

1980
YAMHILL COUNTY
SPARKLING WINE
(24% Pinot noir 76% Chardonnay)
FERMENTED IN THIS BOTTLE

Produced and bottled by Arterberry Ltd. BW-OR-75 McMinnville, Oregon
Grapes grown by Jim and Lois Maresh, Dundee, Oregon

Serve well chilled
Alcohol 12% by volume. 750 ml.

Arterberry Ltd.
P.O. Box 772
905 E. 10th Street
McMinnville, Oregon 97128
(503) 472-1587

Arterberry Ltd. has the distinction of producing Oregon's first sparkling wine from traditional Champagne grape varieties. Although low alcohol sparkling cider has been Arterberry's commercial staple, Fred Arterberry, a winemaking graduate from U.C. Davis, is dedicated to the production of premium sparkling wines from Chardonnay and Pinot Noir.

Arterberry, like all sparkling beverage producers, is forced to contend with absurd taxation laws. Still wine is taxed at the rate of 17 cents a gallon, but sparkling wine, classified as a luxury item, is taxed at twenty times that rate, at $3.40 a gallon. Even Arterberry's inexpensive cider is taxed at $2.40 a gallon. As sparkling wine moves through the distribution channels, the tax's impact on the eventual price to the consumer is magnified even further.

Premium sparkling wine is made by adding sugar and yeast to the base wine after it has finished fermentation. The wine is then bottled with temporary closures, and a second fermentation takes place within the bottle. This second fermentation, and the subsequent resting of the wine on the yeast is responsible for the wine's natural carbonation and distinctive character.

Arterberry believes that Oregon is ideal for sparkling wine. If grapes are too high in sugar, the base wine will be too high in alcohol, and the second fermentation cannot take place. Grapes for sparkling wine must be picked at lower sugar levels. In warmer climates, grapes ripen at higher sugar levels, and although picking the grapes early allows a sparkling wine to be made, it does little for quality. In Oregon's cooler climate, grapes fully ripen at lower sugars, an important criterion for premium sparkling wines. Arterberry prefers grapes at 20 degrees Brix, a sugar level that produces a base wine with an alcohol content of about 11 percent.

The first cuvee was 100 percent Chardonnay from the 1979 vintage. Subsequent cuvees have included Pinot Noir. The wines remain on the yeast for up to two years, and are then sealed with a Champagne style cork, a practice that requires a special corking machine.

In 1982, to augment his sparkling wine production, Arterberry made his first table wines for release under the Arterberry label, Chardonnay, Pinot Noir, and Rose of Pinot Noir from the Red Hills Vineyard near Dundee.

Oregon is destined to become an important sparkling wine producing region, and Arterberry has become the first to point the way. Arterberry is open most weekends from 11 AM to 5 PM.

Ellendale Vineyards
300 Reuben Boise Road
Dallas, Oregon 97338
(503) 623-5617

Founded in 1981 by Robert and Ella Mae Hudson, Ellendale Vineyards is located twenty miles west of Salem, and two miles west of Dallas. The first vineyards were planted in 1975, but the local deer population destroyed most of the vines, and the vineyard was replanted and fenced in 1980 and 1981.

While waiting for their 13 acre vineyard to mature, the Hudsons began producing fruit and berry wines, and mead from local honey. Emphasis is shifting to grape wines as more grapes become available from their own vineyards and from local growers. By the mid 80's, the Hudson's expect to reach their planned maximum grape wine production of 15,000 gallons. Ellendale will continue producing some fruit wines, and, in addition to their still grape wines, will make sparkling wines made from Riesling, Chardonnay, and Pinot Noir.

The tasting room is open Wednesday through Sunday from 1 PM to 6 PM. Owner Robert Hudson is a landscape artist, specializing in scenes of Oregon, the Oregon Trail, and other Northwest settings. He has had a number of shows throughout the Northwest, and his works are on display and for sale in the winery's tasting room.

Hood River Vineyards
4693 Westwood Drive Hood River, Oregon 97031
(503) 386-3772

Hood River Vineyards is the first Oregon vinifera grape winery in the modern era to be located somewhere other than west of the Cascade Mountain Range. But that is not to say Hood River is east of the Cascades. The winery and vineyards, in fact, are nestled in a unique microclimate at the intersection of the Cascade Range and the Columbia River.

At this intersection, the opposite climates of eastern and western Oregon collide to form a climatic habitat quite different than either. The soils are a volcanic basalt. The summers are warmer and the winters colder than those of western Oregon's Willamette Valley, and rainfall is less.

Hood River Vineyards is owned and operated by Clifford and Eileen Blanchette. The Blanchettes started making fruit wine from some of the eight acres of pears on their farm. Becoming enthused with Oregon's grape wines, the Blanchettes planted an experimental acre of Riesling in 1974, and increased their grape acreage to the present twelve. Gewurztraminer has been especially promising.

126

Hood River will continue to market Perry, a pear wine, and for the future, the Blanchettes are interested in producing sparkling wine, and putting in a still for fruit brandy. Hood River is open to the public for tasting and tours from May through December, 1 PM to 5:30 PM, every day except Friday.

Serendipity Cellars Winery

15275 Dunn Forest Road
Monmouth, Oregon 97361
(503) 838-4284

Glen and Cheryl Longshore, Serendipity's owners, planted their first grapes in 1980. The vineyard totals only three acres, and there are no plans to increase its size. The Longshores are more interested in winemaking than grape growing. The small vineyard is intended mostly as a way for them to better understand grape growing, and thereby better understand the limitations, problems, and possibilities confronting their growers. A neighbor is planting a vineyard that will eventually be expanded to 30 acres, and the Longshores will be buying some of his grapes on long-term contract.

Pinot Noir is Serendipity's speciality, made not only as a red wine, but also as Pinot Noir Blanc, and a light red wine named Fruite, styled similarly to Beaujolais.

Production is quite limited, and plans call for slow growth to a maximum of 7,500 gallons a year. The winery is open to the public Saturday, 11 AM to 6 PM, and Sunday, 1 PM to 6 PM. May through December, Serendipity is also open Fridays from 11 AM to 6 PM. Those interested in receiving announcements of new releases can write Serendipity and request to be included on their mailing list.

Alcohol 12% by Volume
Produced and Bottled by
Wasson Brothers Winery
Oregon City, Oregon
BW-OR-83

W I N E

Wasson Brothers Winery
19925 South Leland Road
Oregon City, Oregon 97045
(503) 655-3301

The Wasson Brothers Winery has the distinction of being owned and operated by perhaps the only twin brothers in the wine industry. Initially fruit and berry home winemakers, Jim and John Wasson were spurred into the commercial wine business by wine judging successes in the Oregon State Fair. As their hobby grew into a commercial enterprise, winemaking interests shifted more toward premium grape wines.

Both brothers have other full-time employment, coordinating their days off to work at the winery and their small vineyard. The first plantings of Chardonnay, Riesling, and Pinot Noir are being augmented by new plantings of Gewurztraminer and Early Muscat. The vineyard will total ten acres, a fairly modest size, but more than enough to care for during weekends and "vacations."

The Wasson Brothers Winery does not yet have public hours, but expansion is imminent, and the new winery facility will be equipped with a tasting room.

WASHINGTON

Washington Wineries

1. Arbor Crest
2. Associated Vintners Winery
3. Bainbridge Island Winery
4. Chateau Ste. Michelle
5. Daquila Wines
6. E.B. Foote Winery
7. Haviland Vintners
8. Hinzerling Vineyards
9. The Hogue Cellars
10. Kiona Vineyards
11. F.W. Langguth Winery
12. Latah Creek Winery
13. Leonetti Cellar
14. Mont Elise Vineyards
15. Mount Baker Vineyards
16. Neuharth Winery
17. Preston Wine Cellars
18. Quail Run Vintners
19. Quilceda Creek Vintners
20. Salishan Vineyards
21. Paul Thomas Wines
22. Tucker Cellars
23. Vernier Wines
24. Manfred Vierthaler Winery
25. Woodward Canyon Winery
26. Worden's Washington Winery
27. Yakima River Winery

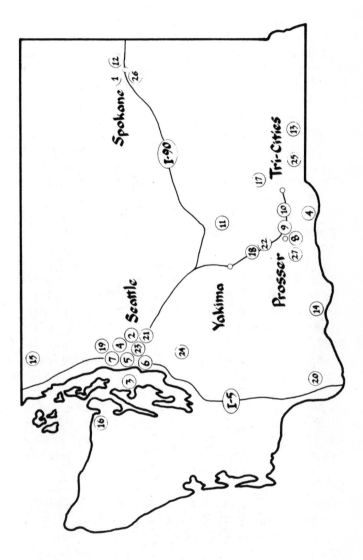

131

THE WINE INDUSTRY

Now America's second largest producer of premium *Vitis vinifera* wine grapes, until the late 1960's, most of Washington's wine industry had little interest in premium wines or wine grapes. Washington was a large producer of grapes, but these were mostly *Vitis labrusca* used for grape juice products or for making indifferent fortified wines. Although the state's wine industry, such as it was, was already established in a sense, what launched the region's biggest wine industry was an unlikely combination of a winewriter, some amateur winemakers, and the removal of protectionist state wine laws at the urging of wine retailers who were openly hostile to the state's wine industry and had little interest in premium wines from the state.

To abbreviate what is a rather elaborate story, a group of amateur winemakers began, in the late 1950's, purchasing grapes from the few vinifera plots that then existed, rescuing them from fortified blends with *Vitis labrusca* grapes. In 1962, to insure a steady supply of grapes, the group purchased vineyard acreage and became a bonded winery, Associated Vintners. In 1966, Leon Adams, the noted authority on American wines, visited Associated Vintners. Impressed with some of their early efforts, Adams suggested that they become a commercial enterprise. In 1967, Associated Vintners produced their first commercial vintage.

With the expected removal of protectionist wine laws, another winery, American Wine Growers, one of the state's largest, and the corporate predecessor of Chateau Ste. Michelle, was becoming interested in developing premium table wines. At the suggestion of Adams, Andre Tchelistcheff, the legendary California winemaker, visited the state, tasted the wines of the two wineries, and ultimately became consultant to American Wine Growers. In 1967, the same year that Associated Vintners "went public," American Wine Growers, under the label Ste. Michelle, produced their first commercial release of *Vitis vinifera* wine.

Until recent years, the Washington wine industry was a paradox, having a relatively large number of grapes, but very few wineries. Most of the wineries were located west of the Cascades, far from the source of the grapes. By the mid 70's, the Wallace family had established Hinzerling Vineyards, a small vineyard and winery in south-central Washington's Yakima Valley. Along the

Columbia River Gorge, the Hendersons, with other partners, founded Bingen Wine Cellars (Mont Elise Vineyards). Near Pasco, on a much larger scale, the Prestons founded Preston Wine Cellars, still the Northwest's largest family-owned winery.

By the early 80's, the Washington wine industry finally had become truly diversified. The largest wineries grew still larger. Many small wineries began operation. New and distinct growing regions entered the scene, and wineries were opening all across the state. Chateau Ste. Michelle planted a single vineyard that stretched, literally, for miles, and the state's wine industry attracted its first foreign money with partial German financing of the F. W. Langguth Winery.

Riesling is the backbone of the Washington wine industry. Consumer demand for white wines, and for semi-sweet white wines in particular, puts Riesling in a dominant position. Washington reliably produces Riesling grapes that are high both in acid and in sugar. No other American winegrowing region can so easily produce good quality Riesling on such a scale. Grape growers are planting new acreage heavily to Riesling.

In establishing a national market, Washington needs to be readily identified with a distinctive type or style of wine, something the state can hang its vinous hat on. Riesling has been and will be the wine. Besides being a very good grape for Washington, it conveniently fits into the nation's popular perception that Washington would likely produce good Riesling since the state is a northern, and therefore, it might be assumed, cooler winegrowing climate.

There are, however, some dangers in the industry's direction. While consumer demand for semi-sweet white wines is high, a large segment of this market is attracted to cheaper wines, and is not necessarily drawn to the higher priced premium Rieslings. Consumer tastes may be changing, broadening, or becoming more "sophisticated," as evidenced by the recent influx European "jug" wines for everyday consumption that are quite dry and relatively higher in acid. Washington could soon find itself with an ample supply of Riesling and Chenin Blanc, but a shortage of the traditionally dry white varieties.

From an enophile's jaded point of view, except for the heavily botrytised sweet "dessert" renditions of the grape, the most important and interesting Washington white wine is not Riesling, but Chardonnay, Sauvignon Blanc, and Semillon. Washington does very well indeed with these varieties.

133

The nation's white wine boom will not last indefinitely. Though largely ignored, Washington's red wines will qualitatively be among the state's most important wines. Grape grower, winemaker, and consumer alike have been long in coming to terms with Washington Cabernet Sauvignon and Merlot, the state's premier red wine grapes. A few wineries are already producing outstanding wine from these varieties, and for many more wineries, success is close at hand. Unlike Oregon, Washington has all the prerequisites for rapid and large-scale expansion. South-central Washington, the state's principal grape growing area, is not densely populated. Choice vineyard land competes less with residential sprawl. Land is relatively cheap, and vast acreage is available and suitable for grape growing.

Large-scale agricultural interests and family-owned farms and ranches form the economic backbone of south-central Washington. When it became clear that premium wine grapes were fast becoming the crop of choice, local farmers and ranchers were quick to respond. The openness of the land invites farming, or grape growing, on a large scale. It is not surprising, then, that once the winegrowing boom got started, vineyard and winery expansion came on with a rush.

Had the coming of age of Washington wines begun earlier, say in the 70's, the expansion of the Washington wine industry would have been even more astounding. A lot of Washington wine will be entering the marketplace at a time when domestic wine production is increasing and sales are flattening out. Washington wineries are producing far too much wine to be sold locally, yet few are experienced with promoting and selling wine outside the state. Winegrowers are becoming cautious in their expansion, planting fewer grapes and making less wine than they otherwise might. The industry's growth, nevertheless, is still tremendous. Washington's complete dominance of the non-California premium American wine market may be only slightly delayed.

WINEGROWING CLIMATES

Washington's major winegrowing region is located in the Columbia Basin in the south-central portion of the state. Most of the grape growing sites have heat unit ranges similar to Burgundy or Bordeaux at a latitude that falls between the two famous French regions. Yet to merely state this and say no more grossly over-simplifies the climatic nature of the region.

As a winegrowing climate, the Columbia Basin is unique. Pacific marine air is blocked by the towering Cascade Mountain Range, leaving south-central Washington in a rain shadow that reaches to the eastern part of the state. It is an arid environment. Much of the area receives less than ten inches of rain a year. Except near rivers and streams, the land is naturally treeless. Grasses and sagebrush are the most common vegetation.

With so little rainfall, the land is a virtual desert, yet with irrigation, the Columbia Basin is transformed into a rich agricultural region. In many respects, it is an ideal winegrowing climate. Under cloudless skies, warm sunny days are followed by cool clear nights. Because of the northerly latitude, day length is longer during the growing season. Rain during harvest is rare. Winter freezing presents the only major critical problem for grape growers, but better viticultural practices have greatly lessened the danger.

Increases in grape sugar are dependent on warmth and sunlight, and the long sunny days insure ample sugars at harvest. The grapes are not low in acid, however, like those grown in sunny southerly climates. Acid reduction is mostly dependent on temperature, but increases in sugar depend on both temperature and sunlight, so the combination of cool nights and long sunny days insures that the grapes have adequate acid even at relatively high sugar levels.

Many of a winegrowing region's characteristics can be both problems and opportunities for the winegrower. Europeans work with grapes that tend to be low in sugar and high in acid, Californians with grapes that tend to be high in sugar and low in acid. Winegrowers in south-central Washington work with grapes that can be abundant in both sugar and acid. Although this is one of the region's assets, there is sometimes too much of a good thing. One of the challenges for the Washington wine industry has been to develop viticultural practices to insure that the grapes will not be simultaneously overripe with too high an acid content, and to develop winemaking practices to handle grapes with these tendencies.

South-central Washington is the Northwest's most versatile winegrowing region. More varieties grow well in the area than in any other Northwest climate. With proper site selection, virtually all the major grape varieties will ripen, develop good varietal flavors, and maintain desired acid levels. And as a bonus, warm days of sunshine, nighttime cooling, and the control of moisture through irrigation provide an excellent climatic environment for sweet botrytised wines.

Vineyards can be pruned for modest yields for premium wines, yet because the climate allows high yields while maintaining good acid balance and varietal definition, the region lends itself well to the production of premium "jug" wines. One winery accidentally allowed a block of Chenin Blanc to yield over 15 tons an acre. The juice had good sugar and acid balance, and the vines produced normally the following year. The large blocks of land available for cultivation and the typically gentle slopes make mechanical harvesting easily feasible. Premium wines, however, gave birth to Washington's modern wine industry, and premium wines continue to be the industry's foundation as well as its glory.

The Columbia Basin itself covers thousands of square miles. Only a very small portion has been developed for grape growing. The growing climate is so unique and the region so diverse that its full potential is scarcely known and may not really be understood for decades.

The Yakima Valley is the most geographically distinct of the present major growing areas, and in the spring of 1983, the Yakima Valley became Washington's first approved American Viticultural Area. Separated from the rest of the Columbia Basin by a series of ridges and small mountain ranges called the Yakima Folds, much of the Valley is slightly cooler and more temperate than the growing sites to the east. As a general rule, the Yakima Valley becomes cooler as one moves further north and west. Among the Yakima Valley wineries are Hinzerling, Kiona, Yakima River, Quail Run, Hogue, and Tucker.

Other major Columbia Basin growing sites include the area north of Pasco in the wide "U" of land formed by the confluence of the Columbia and Snake Rivers, and areas further north and south along the Columbia River from Mattawa to Paterson, areas such as the Wahluke Slope, Cold Creek Valley, and Paterson Ridge. Langguth, Preston, and Chateau Ste. Michelle's River Ridge winery are located in this broad growing region, and large vineyards populate the area, supplying the grapes for many of Washington's wineries. Sagemoor Farms, the Northwest's largest independent grape grower, not only supplies grapes to Washington wineries, but to wineries in Idaho and Oregon as well. Further to the east, on the state's southern border, the Walla Walla Valley is emerging as a notable grape growing area with the Leonetti and Woodward Canyon wineries.

Spokane area wineries using primarily Columbia Basin grapes from south-central Washington include Arbor Crest, Worden's, and Latah Creek. Wineries west of the Cascades, primarily in the Seattle area, using mostly south-central Washington grapes include Associated Vintners, Chateau Ste. Michelle, E. B. Foote, Paul Thomas, Daquila, Haviland, Neuharth, Quilceda, and Vernier.

Although the Washington wine industry is dominated by the south-central growing region, other areas are developing. Among them, Mont Elise in Bingen, Washington specializes in Pinot Noir and Gewurztraminer grown in a discrete microclimate on the Columbia River Gorge where the Columbia River cuts through the Cascade Range, and the climates of eastern and western Washington converge and collide.

Though cooler and wetter than most of western Oregon, that state's major winegrowing area, western Washington is emerging as a notable, if not large-scale, winegrowing area. In southwest Washington, near the Oregon border, in a climate similar to Oregon's Willamette Valley, Salishan is focusing on Pinot Noir. Further north, near Seattle, in the cooler, wetter Puget Sound area, Manfred Vierthaler and Bainbridge Island are working with Muller-Thurgau and other cool climate grape varieties, and further north still, in a relatively warm microclimate near the Canadian border, Mt. Baker is engaged in extensive work with numerous cool climate varieties.

GRAPE VARIETIES

Washington has two distinct and radically different growing climates, the major grape growing climate east of the Cascade Mountain Range in south-central Washington, and the much cooler and wetter climate west of the Cascades. At present, only miniscule quantities of grapes are grown in western Washington, and the varieties that do well there are, for the most part, quite different from the varieties grown east of the Cascades. In terms of sheer quantity and impact on the marketplace, the grape varieties grown in south-central Washington dominate the state's wine industry. Unless otherwise noted, the discussion of grape varieties pertains to the south-central growing climate.

CABERNET SAUVIGNON, now an outstanding Washington varietal, has not been the easiest grape to tame. The potential of Cabernet Sauvignon was evident from the earliest years, but excellence was long in coming. The first wines did not go through malolactic fermentation, a virtual necessity for quality Washington Cabernet Sauvignon. The grape variety itself is prone to high pH, and careful selection of growing sites is important to the success of the wine.

Washington Cabernets are typically full bodied, moderately high in alcohol, rough, tannic, and inaccessible when young, frequently requiring several years bottle aging to begin showing well. Because the best are frequently hard, relatively high in acid, and unyielding in their youth, they have often been misunderstood by winemaker and consumer alike. To make the wines more drinkable sooner, winemakers have sometimes been inclined to dilute some of the essential strengths of the wine to its inevitable detriment. Happily, Cabernet Sauvignon is now much better understood, and though not all Washington Cabernets yet reflect this better understanding, some excellent wines are on the market, and many more are in the barrel. The 80's promise to be the decade for Washington Cabernet Sauvignon.

CHARDONNAY makes excellent wine, though it has proven to be one of the most difficult white varietals for winegrowers. The grape ripens without difficulty, but at the same time is sometimes quite high in acid, challenging both the grape grower and winemaker. Most now have a handle on the grape, and Washington Chardonnays are reliably good and often excellent. Unlike Oregon, few Washington winemakers put Chardonnay through malolactic fermentation, preferring more of the fruit of the grape rather than the alternate complexities offered by the secondary fermentation. If not always the easiest wine to make, Chardonnay has proven to be among the most rewarding.

CHENIN BLANC produces high yields with good sugar and acid balance. Usually finished semi-dry, the wines are quite pleasant, if not particularly distinguished.

GEWURZTRAMINER does exceptionally well. One of the state's early successes, Gewurztraminer helped make a name for Washington white wine. Dry Gewurztraminers are an ideal match for more aggressive food courses. This is not to say that all Washington Gewurztraminers are exceptional. The grape is fickle and must be picked at just the right ripeness. Picked too early, the spicy varietal character is lost. Picked too late, the wine is heavy, flat, dull, and bitter. Cooler growing sites are usually best. Unlike other grape varieties grown in the state, cane rather than cordon pruning is often recommended.

GRENACHE, a pleasant, fairly flavorful, red wine grape, and a traditional candidate for rose, is grown only in small quantities in the warmest growing sites. Its erratic crops and sensitivity to winter cold do not endear it to winegrowers.

LEMBERGER, sometimes spelled Limberger, is a little known red wine grape grown in small quantities in several European countries. Best known as a wine from the Wurttemberg region of Germany, the grape came to Washington from Hungary via British Columbia in the late 30's as part of Washington State University's research program. Dr. Walter Clore, horticulturist emeritus from Washington State University, worked with the grape from the early years and has long been an ardent advocate. Winemakers, however, have been much less enthused, in part, because of the inherent marketing problems for an unknown variety with a name reminiscent of a foul smelling cheese.

Lemberger has been called Washington's Zinfandel, a characterization not too far from the truth. Lemberger adapts to a wide range of styles from light and fruity to big and tannic. It does well in most south-central Washington growing sites, has naturally low pH, yields six tons or more an acre, and, after the vines have established their root systems, is quite winter-hardy. Lemberger has sufficient character and interest to justify bottling as a "premium wine," yet, cropped higher, Lemberger is an excellent candidate for good quality "jug wines." At present, Washington has very little acreage planted to the grape.

MADELEINE ANGEVINE, a cool climate variety, is grown only in western Washington where it ripens well and yields abundant fruit.

MERLOT, one of the Bordeaux grape varieties, when grown outside its homeland, is often either light and lacking in intensity or else "big," but low acid and one dimensional. The inherently higher acidity of Washington Merlot complements the grape. The best Washington Merlots are full-bodied but tightly structured wines of distinction. Merlot can easily become overripe, however, and must be carefully monitored as harvest approaches. Washington Merlots are reliably good, and the best are excellent.

MULLER-THURGAU, a high yielding and early ripening variety similar in general character to Riesling, is one of the principal varieties grown in the cool climates west of the Cascades.

OKANAGAN RIESLING, a traditional Canadian wine grape, is making its way south into western Washington. Once of mysterious origin, the grape is now known to be a hybrid and not a true vinifera.

PINOT NOIR, according to latitude and heat unit measurements, should have been a good grape for south-central Washington. Regrettably, the wines are seldom distinguished, and are usually no more successful than most California Pinot Noirs. Very little new acreage is being devoted to the grape. Occasionally there have been significant successes, however, and it is premature to entirely dismiss south-central Washington Pinot Noir.

Some of Washington's secondary growing areas such as the Columbia River Gorge and selected sites in the western part of the state produce very fine Pinot Noir, though as yet in very small quantities, and it is likely that other Washington growing sites will emerge.

RIESLING, also known as White Riesling and Johannisberg Riesling, is the state's most widely planted variety. Washington Rieslings are typically riper and fuller bodied than those from Oregon. Although the grape has become a bread-and-butter mainstay of Washington's wine industry, Riesling has also been responsible for very fine ice and botrytised wines. Because Washington Riesling maintains good acidity even at high sugar levels, some winegrowers make Riesling quite sweet, but except for the special ice and botrytised wines, Washington Rieslings are at their best when they are made less ripe and less sweet, letting the delicacy and balance of the grape carry through.

SAUVIGNON BLANC, also known as Fume Blanc, does very well, yielding wines with a typically pronounced, grassy, varietal character. Nationally, the grape has gained increasing favor in recent years, and Washington offers fine examples for those who enjoy the more pronounced varietal renditions of the grape.

SEMILLON, a genetic relative of Sauvignon Blanc, and, in America, usually a grape of modest distinction and interest, does far better in Washington than its reputation, yielding flavorful wines with pronounced grassy flavors similar to Sauvignon Blanc. For those who enjoy its aggressive character, Washington produces some of the best.

WASHINGTON
WINERIES

SAUVIGNON BLANC
1982
BACCHUS VINEYARD

PRODUCED AND BOTTLED BY
WASHINGTON CELLARS, SPOKANE, WASHINGTON
ALCOHOL 12.0% BY VOLUME

Arbor Crest

Founded 1982
East 4506 Buckeye, Spokane, Washington 99207
(509) 484-WINE

Daily, Noon to 5:30 PM.

ARBOR CREST

The Mielke family has been in the agricultural business in the Spokane area for three generations. The 100 acre farm, owned by two brothers, Dave and Harry Mielke, produces pie cherries, and fresh vegetables for local sale. Harry Mielke, a research hemotologist, had long been interested in wine, and in the late 70's, an experimental vineyard was planted on the farm. The six acre vineyard includes more than 40 varieties of vinifera, native American, and French-American hybrids.

Interest in grape growing stimulated interest in a winery, and in 1982, the Mielkes hired Scott Harris, a U. C. Davis graduate in enology, and then assistant winemaker at California's Davis Bynum winery. The cherry processing operations were moved to other buildings on the farm, and winemaking equipment was moved in.

Twenty-four thousand gallons of wine were made that first year. Production will rapidly increase to the operation's 50,000 gallon capacity. For a winery of its size, Arbor Crest is generously well equipped with a centrifuge and an advanced laboratory for wine analysis.

Grapes are purchased from several grape growers, primarily from Sagemoor Farms near Pasco, but in Spring of 1983, a partnership joined by Arbor Crest planted 66 acres of grapes on the Wahluke Slope near Mattawa. When the vineyard begins bearing commercial crops, Arbor Crest will be able to supply most of its own grapes.

Focus is mainly on Riesling and Chardonnay, but Sauvignon Blanc, Gewurztraminer, Cabernet Sauvignon, and Merlot wines are produced as well. Most of the production is in white wine, reflecting current consumer interests. The wines for wood aging will see only French oak.

The Cabernet is made in a style meant for long aging. The skins and pulp are not removed until the wine has finished fermentation. It is then aged for two years in French oak, mostly Never, and another two years in the bottle before release, a long and costly wait for a new winery.

Commercial winemaking is not just a hobby, it is a business, and of necessity, there is concern for maximizing profits. Everything becomes a trade off between what is desireable, and what is com-

Scott Harris tastes new Chardonnay from the barrel.

mercially feasible. The decision to use more expensive French oak as opposed to American oak is one example of this trade off, American oak devotees not withstanding.

The use of press wine is another one, of many, areas of compromise. The grape variety, growing region, vintage, and type of wine press all play roles in determining the ideal gallons- per-ton yield. The free run juice that is yielded after the grapes are crushed but before they are pressed is the proverbial cream of the crop, but inclusion of some press wine is usually desireable (and economically necessary), up to a point. Heavier pressings yield more juice per ton, but also release harsh phenolics and other flavors that detract from the wine's character. Arbor Crest presses Chardonnay for a yield of less than 150 gallons per ton, and Riesling for 130 gallons per ton, moderate yields, especially for sophisticated wine presses.

For years, Seattle area wineries in the more cosmopolitan western part of the state have dominated the Washington wine industry. Arbor Crest is among the new wave of Spokane area wineries adding balance and diversity to the states burgeoning wine industry.

THE ASSOCIATED VINTNERS

1980
WASHINGTON STATE
CABERNET SAUVIGNON

VINTED AND BOTTLED BY THE ASSOCIATED VINTNERS
BELLEVUE, WASHINGTON B.W. 56 ALCOHOL 13% BY VOLUME

Associated Vintners
Founded 1962
1445 120th Avenue N.E., Bellevue, Washington 98005
(206) 453-1977

Tuesday through Saturday, 11 AM to 4 PM;
Sunday, Noon to 4 PM.

ASSOCIATED VINTNERS

Associated Vintners has expanded greatly since its early beginnings. By 1982, twenty years after the small collective of home winemakers formed a tiny commercial winery, the first in the modern era dedicated to the cause of premium Washington vinifera grape wines, production had grown to 90,000 gallons a year, nearing the 120,000 gallon capacity of Associated Vintners' new winery, the fourth in their twenty year history of growth.

The beginnings of Associated Vintners are legendary. In the early 1950's, Lloyd Woodburne, then a professor of psychology at the University of Washington, began making homemade wine. Interest spread among Woodburne's colleagues, and it was not long before a number of the University of Washington faculty were buying grapes and making wine. The group decided to band together and purchase a power grape crusher that Woodburne would keep in his garage. In order to avoid violating legal strictures, the group formed a corporation, and in 1962, became a bonded winery— Associated Vintners.

In 1966, the noted wine authority, Leon Adams, tasted one of Woodburne's Grenache roses, found it excellent, and suggested that Associated Vintners ought to become a commercial winery. In 1967, the most famous and respected of all American winemakers, Andre Tchelistcheff, tasted a Gewurztraminer made by Phil Church, another home winemaker in the group, and considered it the best Gewurztraminer made in the United States. Spurred by this enthusiastic response, Associated Vintners, in 1967, moved the crusher from Woodburne's garage to a small facility in Kirkland, Washington, a suburb of Seattle, and produced their first commercial vintage.

Phil Church, a meteorologist, and one of the original ten shareholders, made early studies of Washington's climates, showing, among other things, that parts of Washington east of the Cascades have virtually the same heat units as parts of France's Burgundy region. Although it is now recognized that heat unit measurements are only a partial indication of viticultural comparability, Church's early studies provided much of the impetus for vinifera grape growing in Washington. Woodburne emphasizes that Church, now deceased, deserves much credit for the pioneering

Leading founder of Associated Vintners, Lloyd Woodburne.

work that helped launch Washington's rapidly growing wine industry.

Associated Vintners has undergone many changes over the years. In 1976, the winery moved from its small building in Kirkland to a much larger, more modern facility in nearby Redmond. By 1980, production had increased to 25,000 gallons a year, and it was becoming increasingly clear that Associated Vintners was, in many ways, outgrowing itself. The time had come for a transformation to preserve and enhance the vitality of the original enterprise without compromising its fundamental and sustaining spirit. New capital was generated by selling the winery's vineyards and increasing the number of shareholders to 30. Included in the new group are key members with business and marketing expertise.

In 1981, Associated Vintners moved to the adjacent community of Bellevue, to a facility three times the size of the Redmond winery. Better equipment was purchased. The old, horizontal, white wine, fermenting tanks were largely replaced by modern, temperature controlled vertical tanks, and the wines became fresher, less prone to oxidation, and retained more of their fruit.

Wines were no longer aged, bottled, and released by an arbitrary schedule, but according to the character of the variety and the vintage. Many of Associated Vintners' wines benefit from lengthy aging, but those that do not are released earlier, while they retain their fresh and lively character.

Winemaker David Lake has played a key role in Associated Vintners' transformation. Lake holds what is undoubtedly the wine world's most distinguished title—Master of Wine from Britain's Institute of Masters of Wine. Although the institute has been in existence for some 30 years, only about 100 persons have been certified as Masters of Wine. Lake came to the United States after ten years in the British wine trade. He studied for a year at the University of California at Davis, and worked for a time at Eyrie in Oregon with David Lett, who subsequently recommended him to Woodburne.

Whether consumer or member of the wine trade, the majority of us become most familiar with a particular wine style and tend to judge all other wines against that frame of reference. Lake brings a unique perspective to the Washington wine scene. By definition, as a Master of Wine, Lake has developed a highly eclectic palate, an in depth familiarity with the diverse wines and wine styles of the world. In his view, there has been too much of a tendency to down play some of the distinctive characteristics of Washington wines, attempts to mold them into more familiar wine styles, to the detriment of the wine and the winegrowing region. There is a growing trend, he notes, for Washington winemakers to allow the wines be themselves, a trend that has done much to further the quality of Washington wines and advance the region's state of the art.

Associated Vintners does not always release wines sequentially, but in accordance with the vintage and character of the wine. Wines from lighter, fruity vintages may be released earlier than wines with a deeper structure that need and benefit from lengthier aging. Lake does not attempt to level out the differences from vintage to vintage to create a uniform "house style" by bolstering lighter vintages, or, figuratively speaking, watering down classic wines from outstanding vintages that happen to be hard and inaccessible in their youth. Strengths are not minimized for the sake of uniformity, and excellence is not sacrificed at the alter of cash flow and immediate consumer appeal.

Complementary wine batches may be blended to make a superior wine, but when warranted, wine batches are kept separate,

Winemaker, David Lake.

and released under single vineyard appelations. Some less expensive wines, or those meant for earlier consumption, are released under the Columbia Cellars label.

Lake admits that he was uncomfortable with the sale of the winery's vineyards, and the loss of immediate and direct control over the grapes. In retrospect, however, things have worked well. Grapes are abundant. The best can be selected from among the best sites, and the winery is not locked into a single growing area for all their wines when other sites would produce some varieties better. Lake insists on pH readings as well as sugar and acid figures when buying grapes. As harvest approaches, Lake visits the growers at least once a week, looking at the condition of the vineyards, and tasting the grapes. Sugar, acid, and pH readings do not tell the whole story, and tasting the grapes, particularly Gewurztraminer, Riesling, and Semillon, gives important indications of ripeness, quality, and character.

The taste of Gewurztraminer is not for everyone, and it is not an easy wine to make well, but Associated Vintners has justly earned a reputation for this variety, made in a dry Alsatian style. Lake likens south-central Washington's arid growing environment to France's Alsace region, noting that the drier areas of Alsace produce the best Gewurztraminer. Many American growing regions, including some in the Northwest, produce Gewurztraminer with a floral, perfumy, and sometimes almost a chewing gum-like flavor. Lake particularly likes Washington's Yakima Valley for Gewurztraminer, feeling that the wines are more tightly structured and spicy, along classic Alsatian lines.

Semillon is becoming another Associated Vintners' specialty. A largely ignored variety, Associated Vintners has demonstrated the grape's potential in Washington state. Lake makes the wine in an intensely varietal rendition of the grape, with a pronounced, crisp, grassy aroma and taste. In Lake's opinion, nowhere else in the world does Semillon produce such a distinctive and flavorful wine of such high quality.

Lake believes that Washington red wine is just now becoming understood, by both consumer and winemaker. In their "natural state," Washington red wines are often tannic, hard, and, in their youth, not particularly friendly to the palate. Washington winemakers have had rapid feedback on what they were doing right and wrong with their white wines, but young Washington red wines are much harder to assess, and without a lengthy regional history of winemaking practices to draw upon, the implications of winemaking decisions were not always immediately apparent.

With a number of vintages under their enological belts, Washington winemakers are now in a much better position to assess the wines and strive for excellence. At the same time, consumers are learning that the the best Washington red wines are not always those that are the most immediately accessible, and that patience in cellaring the wines is well rewarded. A better understanding by both winemaker and consumer is needed. Lake's considerable success with Associated Vintners' red wines, particularly those meant for lengthy cellaring, shows he is holding up his end of the bargain.

There have been many changes since a loose association of amateur vintners banded together more than two decades ago, and became instrumental in the birth of Washington's premium wine industry. The founding members can be justly proud of their accomplishment, and confident that Associated Vintners, Washington's oldest, operating, premium grape winery, is well prepared to help lead the way into the next two decades.

PRODUCED AND BOTTLED BY CHATEAU STE. MICHELLE*
B.W. #8 WOODINVILLE, WASHINGTON. ALCOHOL 12% BY VOLUME

Chateau Ste. Michelle
Founded 1967

P.O. Box 1976, 14111 N.E. 145th
Woodinville, Washington 98072
(206) 488-1133
Daily, 10 AM to 4:30 PM.

P.O. Box 752, Paterson, Washington 99345
(509) 875-2311
Wednesday through Sunday, 11:30 AM to 4:30 PM.

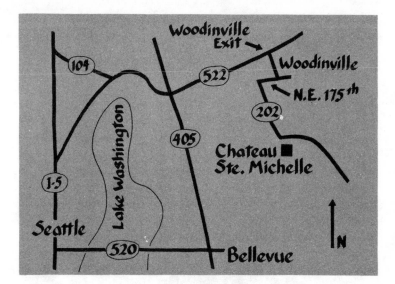

CHATEAU STE. MICHELLE

To most of the wine drinking world, Chateau Ste. Michelle is synonymous with Washington wine. Far larger than any other Northwest winery, and distributed in every major metropolitan market in America, Ste. Michelle has become the defacto representative for the wines of Washington. Ste. Michelle's size and marketing clout insures recognition not only for itself, but for the Washington wine industry as a whole. Chateau Ste. Michelle has done much to bring interest and attention to one of America's most important new winegrowing regions.

The roots of Chateau Ste. Michelle can be traced back to the era immediately following Prohibition, when two companies, Nawico and Pommerelle, began producing non-vinifera grape wines. In 1954, the companies merged to form American Wine Growers. In 1967, American Wine Growers made Semillon, Cabernet Sauvignon, Pinot Noir, and Grenache Rose, the winery's first premium vinifera grape wines, and the first to bear the Ste. Michelle name. In 1973, a group of local investors headed by Wallace Opdycke purchased American Wine Growers. The follow-

Chateau Ste. Michelle's Woodinville winery.

ing year, Ste. Michelle became a wholly owned subsidiary of the United States Tobacco Company.

The massive infusion of capital by Chateau Ste. Michelle's parent company has, within a decade, transformed the winery into one of America's major premium wineries. From a production of 15,000 gallons in 1967, Ste. Michelle has grown to a production of nearly a million gallons a year. Before the decade is out, Ste. Michelle will have doubled in size to two million gallons.

Chateau Ste. Michelle's showcase winery, built in 1976, is located near the community of Woodinville, not far from the city of Seattle. Built on the 87 acre estate once owned by Seattle lumberman Fred Stimson, the attractive chateau-style building houses corporate offices and visitor facilities. Scarcely visible from the winery grounds, the 140,000 square foot production facility is set on a lower plane, preserving the estate's pastoral ambience. The grounds, designed in the early 1900s by the Olmstead brothers of Boston, designers of New York's Central Park and Seattle's Aboretum, have been preserved, and are open to the public. The

154

River Ridge in Paterson.

Stimson home, a National Historical Monument, is available to groups for wine tastings. Approximately 150,000 visit Ste. Michelle's Woodinville winery each year.

As large as the Woodinville winery must have seemed when it was first built, Ste. Michelle rapidly outgrew it. Since all of Ste. Michelle's grapes come from south-central Washington, east of the Cascade Mountains, it was logical for Ste. Michelle to expand their winemaking operations nearer the source of their grapes. Ste. Michelle's first expansion included refurbishing the old Nawico winery at Grandview in the Yakima Valley. The winery's open top tanks were well suited for fermenting red wines, and now all Ste. Michelle's red wines are fermented at Grandview.

The new 25 million dollar River Ridge winery at Paterson, Washington along the Columbia River Gorge is perhaps Chateau Ste. Michelle's boldest move to date. Nearly three times the size of the Woodinville winery, it symbolizes not only Ste. Michelle's commitment to Washington wine, but the economic confidence of Ste. Michelle's parent company in the success of the enterprise,

The central pumping station.

and correlatively, affirmation of the importance of Washington wine in the future of the American wine scene.

For the River Ridge "winery estate," Ste. Michelle planted a new 1,780 acre vineyard adjacent to the winery. The vineyard's unique irrigation system is patterned after traditional agricultural practices of the area. The vines, planted in circular vineyards of roughly 100 acres each, are watered by center-pivot irrigation systems. Irrigation pipe is suspended above the vines on mobile towers on wheels, and, like the hand of a clock, the irrigation pipe and its sprinkler heads sweeps across the circular vineyard, irrigating the vines as it passes. Chateau Ste. Michelle is moving toward increased direct control of their grape supply, and the new River Ridge vineyard is a major step in this direction.

Much of the winemaking area at River Ridge is on a lower level, partially underground. That only a small part of the winery is now in use underscores the magnitude of growth Chateau Ste. Michelle will experience in the next few years. This is not to say that the winery resembles a tank farm at an oil refinery in the fashion of some of California's largest "premium" wineries. Though large-scale by Northwest standards, the fermentation tanks are no bigger than 12,000 gallons, and some are only a quarter that size. Smaller tanks offer the opportunity to treat separate lots of grapes differently, make different blends from the separate lots, or simply

Long racks of oak barrels for aging red wine.

to sell a distinctive batch of wine as a special bottling. River Ridge is by no means merely a cold sterile production facility. Designed in a rustic country estate architectural style, River Ridge features tours and a finely furnished visitor area, retail store, and tasting room.

From a winemaking standpoint, Chateau Ste. Michelle does not conceive itself as a monolithic entity, but rather as an aggregate of several specialized wineries. Peter Bachman, formerly of Monterey Vineyard in California, is director of winemaking operations. Cheryl Barber is winemaker at Woodinville, Doug Gore at Grandview, and Kay Simon at River Ridge. The River Ridge winery produces Ste. Michelle's blended wines for the Farron Ridge label, and specializes in Riesling, Chenin Blanc, and other white varietals not requiring oak aging. River Ridge also crushes Chardonnay and Sauvignon Blanc grapes, clarifies the juice, and sends it to Woodinville for fermentation and wood aging. After fermentation, Grandview also sends its red wines to Woodinville to age in oak.

Until recently, all Ste. Michelle's Cabernet Sauvignon and Merlot were aged in American oak. In 1978, Ste Michelle released its second reserve bottling of Cabernet Sauvignon, their first red wine aged entirely in French oak. The wine was very successful, and the French oak played a significant role in enhancing the character of the wine. Beginning in 1981, Ste. Michelle began putting some of its "regular" Cabernet and Merlot in French oak. With each successive year, French oak will comprise an increasing percentage of the cooperage.

For Washington, and for Chateau Ste. Michelle, consistent success with red wine was long in coming, but by the late 70's, much had been learned about growing the grapes and making the wine. Selecting the right growing site is particularly critical for Cabernet Sauvignon. The site needs to be warm, yet the grapes must maintain good acidity and low pH. Ste. Michelle's best Cabernet grapes routinely come from their Cold Creek Vineyard in the Rattlesnake Hills. The vineyard has a very slight 5 degree southerly slope and receives an average 3,300 heat units during its 210 day growing season.

Development of the red wines dates back to Ste Michelle's inception. In 1967, Andre Tchelistcheff, the legendary California winemaker, visited American Wine Growers, the corporate predecessor to Chateau Ste. Michelle, to discuss Washington's future in the premium wine industry. Tchelistcheff agreed to act as special consultant, and to this day continues in that role, visiting Ste. Michelle four times a year.

From the beginning, Tchelistcheff advocated a "secondary," malolactic fermentation for Ste. Michelle's red wines. This secondary bacterial fermentation converts malic acid to less acidic lactic acid, softening and rounding the wine, and contributing to its complexity. In 1974, Chateau Ste. Michelle achieved their first complete malolactic fermentation, marking an important turning point in the quality of their red wines.

Riesling, made with some residual sugar, is by far Ste. Michelle's most popular wine. While other grape varieties took some learning and development, Ste. Michelle's Rieslings were very good from the start, and immediately appealing to a broad spectrum of consumers. In terms of quantity of production, Riesling continues to play a dominant role at Ste. Michelle.

To the dedicated enophile, however, Chateau Ste. Michelle's other wines are becoming increasingly noteworthy. The dry white table wines have done particularly well in recent years, and the 80's promises to be the decade when Cabernet Sauvignon and Merlot "come of age."

Both the Chardonnay and Fume Blanc are partially fermented in French oak tanks or barrels, then aged briefly in oak prior to bottling. In 1978, the Chardonnay was put through a malolactic fermentation, but since then, Ste. Michelle has emphasized the fruit of the grape, and the Chardonnay is no longer put through the secondary fermentation.

Ste. Michelle was born more than a decade and a half ago with the release of a Semillon-Blanc. The Semillon grape has not been one that garners much attention, but Washington Semillon has proven exceptionally distinctive, perhaps the best Semillon grown anywhere, and Ste. Michelle's Semillon-Blanc has become one of the winery's specialities. In years when a particularly good lot of Semillon is made, the wine is set aside for wood aging and the "Reserve"designation. A genetic relative of Sauvignon Blanc (also called Fume Blanc), Semillon displays similar crisp, grassy-herbaceous flavors.

Chateau Ste. Michelle is a dynamic enterprise, constantly changing itself to meet its own changing needs. In 1983, Chateau Ste. Michelle president Wallace Opdycke resigned his post to pursue his many other business interests. A specialist in finance, Opdycke played the principal role in acquiring a faltering winery in Seattle's industrial district, and within a decade, transforming Chateau Ste. Michelle into the dominant showcase for Northwest wine, developing new vineyards and wineries, and setting the stage for Chateau Ste. Michelle to become a major force in the American wine scene.

In recent years, Ste. Michelle has been acquiring experienced and highly successful sales and marketing personnel from large well-established wineries. New president, Henry Schones, a marketing specialist, will oversee Ste. Michelle's national marketing drive and the winery's in-depth penetration of all major American markets.

Chateau Ste. Michelle's tremendous expansion is taking place at a time when the domestic wine market is flattening out and some wineries are going through difficult times, but Ste. Michelle has overcome much in its brief existence, and its extensive preparation suggests that failure is not an issue, only the magnitude of success.

Chateau Ste. Michelle is putting Washington on the vinous map, and the Washington wine industry as a whole will benefit. By the end of the 80's, Washington will be firmly established in the American wine scene, and Chateau Ste. Michelle will have done much to pave the way.

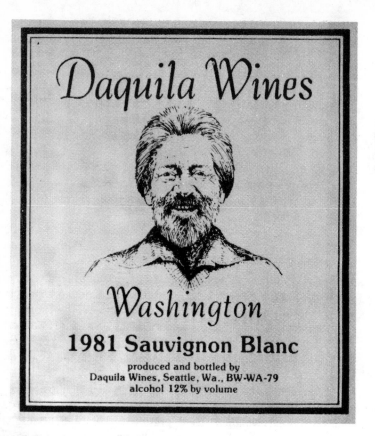

Daquila Wines

Founded 1981
1434 Western Avenue, Seattle, Washington 98101
(206) 343-9521

Friday, 1 PM to 5 PM; Saturday, 10 AM to 5 PM. Call for additional hours during the summer months.

DAQUILA WINES

Frank Daquila has been a winemaker for more than five decades. At the age of twelve, Daquila, a native of Italy, began helping his father make the family wine. A musician, and owner of Seattle's Scandia Music Center, Daquila had long dreamed of owning his own winery. In 1981, the day before his 65th birthday, Daquila began crushing the grapes for his first commercial vintage.

Located just below Seattle's historic Pike Place Market, Daquila's winery is compact, but well equipped with temperature controlled fermentation tanks and a wine lab. Daquila makes Sauvignon Blanc, Semillon, Gewurztraminer, and Merlot. The wines follow his fifty year tradition of winemaking. They are all dry with moderately high acidity—wines that go well with food, wines for the family table.

The Daquila family traditionally served Zinfandel and dry Muscat wines with family meals, and now Gewurztraminer, a grape genetically related to Muscat, is one of Daquila's specialities. Daquila likes Cabernet Sauvignon, but the wines, especially those from Washington, require long aging. Daquila's homemade Cabernet from the 1975 vintage is just now becoming drinkable. For his commercial enterprise, instead of Cabernet, Daquila makes a Merlot, another Bordeaux variety that does very well in Washington, and one that is drinkable much sooner.

Daquila combines modern textbook methods with traditional family winemaking practices. In the fermentation of red wines, most wineries either punch down the floating cap of skins and pulp, or pump the wine back over the cap to break it up and resubmerge it. Daquila keeps the cap continuously submerged by putting a grid over the fermenting wine, a traditional practice in parts of Italy, and a Daquila family winemaking tradition, a practice now adopted by some of the "New World's" boutique wineries.

For most of us, wine is a relatively new hobby, a recently popularized cultural artifact, a civilizing beverage just now becoming part of our lifestyles. For Frank Daquila, this civilizing substance and its association with good food, good company, and the family table harkens back many generations. For Frank Daquila himself, the tradition of winemaking and wine drinking is fifty years deep.

1981

Yakima Valley
Chardonnay
- *Unfiltered*

Produced and Bottled by

e. B. foote winery

Seattle, Washington

Alcohol 13% by Volume
Contents 750 mL

E. B. Foote Winery
Founded 1978
9365 6th Avenue South, Seattle, Washington 98108
(206) 763-9928

Tuesday through Thursday, 6:30 PM to 9 PM; Saturday, 9:30 AM
to 3 PM; or other times by appointment.

E. B. FOOTE WINERY

The E. B. Foote winery started out, in 1978, as a very small, family operation. It is still a family operation, and still quite small, though production has quadrupled since that first year. Gene Foote, a full-time senior engineer at Boeing, is owner and winemaker.

The winery is a natural outgrowth of Foote's interest in wines and winemaking, an interest that started innocently enough with a batch of blackberry wine. Interest in making wine from premium grapes soon followed, and experience with his homemade wines lead Foote to believe he could open a commercial winery and produce some of the best wines in the region.

As Foote says in retrospect, "I got started in commercial winemaking by not knowing what I was getting into. I underestimated what was involved." The first year's production was only 1,300 gallons, but the commitment in time and energy were substantial for a person employed full-time in another occupation. Production has steadily increased, and will continue upward until an estimated 12,000 to 15,000 gallons a year is reached, though further expansion is always a possibility.

Foote makes six wines, Cabernet Sauvignon, Pinot Noir, Chardonnay, Gewurztraminer, Riesling, and Chenin Blanc. All of Foote's grapes come from the Yakima Valley in south-central Washington, most from the Omstead Vineyard near Grandview. Foote prefers Yakima Valley grapes. In his view, they generally have better fruit and balance than grapes from some of the warmer growing areas in the state. Foote emphasizes the importance of high quality fruit. It is a frequently stated maxim that poor wine can be made from outstanding grapes, but outstanding wine can never be made from poor grapes.

Chardonnay is perhaps Foote's best wine. The grapes are harvested to yield about 13½ percent alcohol and an acidity of .75 to .80. The wine is fermented in stainless steel tanks at a temperature of 55 to 60 degrees, then aged in Limousin oak barrels. Foote dislikes the soft unctuous renditions of Chardonnay, preferring a wine not only with substantial body, but a sturdy acid backbone to match. The fairly high acid level balances the wine and makes it a good accompaniment for food. Foote, in fact, makes all his wines to go with food. None are made in a sweet style, and all have enough acidity to refresh the palate throughout a meal.

Gene Foote.

Most winemakers avoid procedures that risk stripping away any of a wine's character, but Foote is more insistent than most in this regard. His wines are rarely fined, and none are filtered. He is able to carry this philosophy through to all his wines, since all are made in a dry style, and without sugar, there is no danger of a few stray yeast cells starting an unwanted fermentation after a wine is bottled. Without fining and filtration, Foote's wines must undergo numerous careful rackings, the process of drawing wine off its sediment, letting it settle over time, and again repeating the process.

In Foote's view, the most important thing a winemaker can do is assign a signature to his wines. If he makes wines that, though good, taste like everyone else's, then he is really not exercising his art. Winemaking is, to be sure, a practiced art, and Foote has done well in developing and refining his own distinctive style—his signature.

1981

HAVILAND VINTNERS

ESTATE BOTTLED

Haviland Vineyard
YAKIMA VALLEY
CABERNET SAUVIGNON

Produced and Bottled by Haviland Vintners
Lynnwood, Washington

ALCOHOL 12% BY VOLUME

Haviland Vintners

Founded 1981
Colony Park Complex, 19029 36th West,
Lynnwood, Washington 98036
(206) 771-6933

Wednesday through Saturday, 11 AM to 3 PM.

HAVILAND VINTNERS

Haviland Vintners, located in the suburbs of Seattle, owns the oldest producing Cabernet Sauvignon vineyard in Washington. Half of the 11 acre vineyard was planted in 1961, the other half in 1965. The vineyard, on a southern slope, over looking the Yakima River, was the source of Chateau Ste. Michelle's first Cabernet Sauvignons.

Most of Haviland's grapes are purchased from other growers, but George DeJarnatt, president and marketing director of Haviland Vintners, feels he is better able to select the best grapes because of his vineyard interests in the area and his contacts with other growers. Before buying grapes, DeJarnatt visits the vineyards, and as harvest approaches, tastes the grapes.

While attending college, DeJarnatt managed a retail wine store. His graduate thesis was on the economics of winery operations, and it had long been his goal to have a winery of his own. After a number of years as an accountant, DeJarnatt left his practice to operate Haviland Vintners. Haviland's purchase of the Cabernet vineyard in 1979 was the initial step that would lead to the founding of the winery.

Bonded in 1981, Haviland made 6,100 gallons of wine that first year, much of it from California grape juice for Haviland's second label, Foret du Mer. Since 1982, all Haviland wines, including their second label, now called Alderwood Cellars, have been made from Washington grapes. Haviland is expanding rapidly, and a yearly production of more than 30,000 gallons is expected soon.

DeJarnatt prefers dry wines to semi-dry or sweet wines, but most of all, he prefers red wines, particularly, Cabernet Sauvignon. Haviland's wine production reflects these preferences. While many new Washington wineries produce almost entirely white wines, primarily semi-sweet Rieslings, Haviland emphasizes dry wines for the table. Haviland does make several Rieslings of varying amounts of residual sugar, but Chardonnay and Sauvignon Blanc are Haviland's most important white wines.

The Chardonnay is aged and partially fermented in French oak. DeJarnatt does not put his Chardonnays through malolactic fermentation, believing that this process, while important for red wines, takes away too much of the Chardonnay complexity. Partially fermenting the Chardonnay in French oak barrels sacrifices

George DeJarnatt.

some of the fruit of the grape as well, but DeJarnatt prefers this slight sacrifice for the richer, fuller quality that barrel fermentation contributes.

While many winemakers are gearing up to ride the white wine boom, DeJarnatt believes that the inevitable transition back toward red wines is already at hand. Cabernet Sauvignon is clearly his most revered wine, but efforts with other red wines have also been notable.

Except for sporadic successes, Pinot Noir from south-central Washington has been no better than average efforts from California. Most Washington Pinot Noir is the Gamay clone, and much of it is grown in warmer growing sites. DeJarnatt has made a small quantity of Pinot Noir from the Pommard clone of the grape, grown in the relatively cooler Yakima Valley. The wine has shown a high quality of fruit and good varietal character. Occasional successes such as this suggest that it is premature to entirely close the books on Pinot Noir from south-central Washington.

Haviland welcomes visitors during the fall crush. Grape deliveries are scheduled for weekends whenever possible, and picnic tables offer a convenient place to sit and view the process. Grapes and fresh juice are available for tasting.

Hínzerlíng

1981   Hinzerling Vineyard

Yakima Valley
GEWÜRZTRAMINER

Produced and Bottled by Hinzerling Vineyards,
Prosser, Wa.

Alcohol 12.5% by volume

Hinzerling Vineyards
Founded 1971
1520 Sheridan Avenue, Prosser, Washington 99350
(509) 786-2163

April through December: Monday through Saturday, 10 AM to Noon and 1 PM to 5 PM; Sunday, Noon to 4 PM. Other times by appointment.

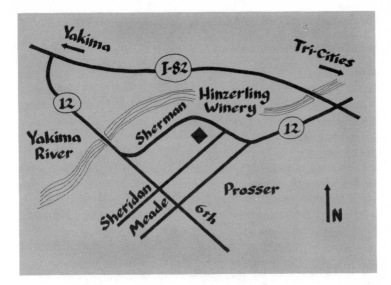

HINZERLING VINEYARDS

In the Yakima Valley at Prosser, Washington, site of Washington State University's Irrigated Agricultural Research and Extension Center, the Wallace family owns and operates the Hinzerling winery and 23 acre vineyard. Mike Wallace and his father Jerry run the day to day operations. Mike is the winemaker.

Locating the winery near the vineyards is not simply a matter of convenience. The Wallace's left behind the temperate climate and cosmopolitan lifestyle of western Washington to be near the source of the grapes. To the Wallaces, grape growing and winemaking are ineluctably intertwined.

The winegrower develops an intimate relationship with the vineyards and the grapes. As vintage follows vintage, he comes to know the subtle variations in the growing season, the response of the vines, and the winemaking adjustments necessary to get the most from the season's grapes. In turn, he acquires a thematic understanding of the wines, and the effects of small adjustments in pruning, training, cropping, irrigating, and harvesting that make the difference between good grapes and the best grapes, and ultimately, the the difference between good wine and the best wine.

It is a corresponsive relationship, quite different from the perspective of a winemaker awaiting delivery of a truckload of purchased grapes from a far away vineyard, knowing the sugar, acid, and pH of the grapes, but little else. For the Wallaces, this is not enough.

In a sense, Hinzerling was Washington's first boutique winery. While some wineries strive, above all, for consistency at the expense of the possibility of excellence, boutique wineries are typically more willing to take risks. The wines, while not always as consistent, can be remarkable, probing the horizons of the winegrowing region.

Hinzerling is the state's foremost producer of botrytised wines. *Botrytis cinerea* is a fungus that, under the right conditions, concentrates the juice of the grapes by reducing their water content, and at the same time, contributing glycerol and flavors of its own to yield an intense, richly sweet wine.

To be beneficial, and not develop into its destructive form, gray rot, *Botrytis cinerea* requires growing conditions uncommon in most of the world's grape growing areas. The Yakima Valley of south-central Washington is one area that offers an unusually ideal climate. Its sandy soil surrenders moisture readily, and the condensation caused by cool night temperatures followed by warm cloudless days offers the right combination of humidity and sunny warmth. Hinzerling's botrytised wines are made from Riesling and Gewurztraminer. According to Mike Wallace, Gewurztraminer is more resistant to Botrytis than Riesling, but just enough so that it is more easily manageable. Hinzerling's most heavily botrytised Gewurztraminer is called Die Sonne, a wine made by picking selected bunches of botrytised grapes and laying them in trays behind the winery. Bees and nighttime condensation help spread the botrytis, further desiccating the grapes and concentrating their essences. The grapes are not crushed until the sugars rise to nearly 40 degrees Brix. The most heavily botrytised Riesling is made not just from selected grape clusters, but from individually hand selected berries.

Neither of these wines are made every year. Because grapes so heavily infected with botrytis yield little juice and involve much hand labor and risk of crop loss, these wines are necessarily expensive, and are sold only in tenths.

The Yakima Valley receives between 2,400 and 2,600 heat units a year. At Hinzerling, bud break occurs between April 15th and April 30th—after the threat of frost has passed. The sandy soil

Mike Wallace.

that benefits botrytis, endangers the vines in winter. Because moisture is released so readily by the sandy soil, winter cold easily penetrates, drying and freezing vulnerable roots. This phenomena is most critical when protective snow covering is lacking, a major factor in the exceptionally destructive winter that followed the 1978 harvest.

Hinzerling's vineyard has suffered little winter damage, partially because of careful protective measures. Irrigation is ceased in August to harden off the vines. Then at harvest, the vines are irrigated to drench the soil and roots, protecting them from drying. Vineyard yield is limited to six tons an acre or less, understressing the vines and allowing them to build a carbohydrate reserve that will later act as protective antifreeze.

Modest yields also preserve the intensity of the grapes so that flavors are not lost in overcropping the vines. Sometimes, however, there can be too much of a good thing. Sacrificing yield and profit margin for quality, Wallace first cropped his Chardonnay vines to a very modest two to three tons an acre. The grapes ripened well and had good acidity—in fact, too much so. By the time the acidity dropped to acceptable levels, the grapes were overripe, and the wines were high in acid, or alcohol, or both. Wallace now crops the Chardonnay at 4½ to 5½ tons an acre. This moves maturity back about ten days, forcing the sugar levels to rise more slowly while the acids drop to the desired levels.

Cabernet Sauvignon has not been the easiest grape for Washington to tame. In the early years, with the exception of some sporadic successes, talk of the potential for excellence was more prevalent than the actuality. Wallace helped point the direction for Washington Cabernets, and was among the first to fully succeed with the grape. Hinzerling's best Cabernets are made from the grapes of their own vineyard. Often rough and tannic when young, the wines need several years of bottle aging to begin showing their best.

In France, Cabernet Sauvignon, Bordeaux's premier grape, is almost always blended with other related varieties. Merlot is the best known of these, but there are others. Wallace has experimented with Malbec and Cabernet Franc. Cabernet Franc, he reports, is quite similar to Cabernet Sauvignon, though not as intense and flavorful. Malbec, on the other hand, is distinctive, combining pleasant herbaceous flavors with scents of violets and lavender. Malbec berries are large, and the clusters are straggly, a result of the variety's typically uneven berry set. Malbec is naturally high in malic acid. Experimental blends of Malbec and Cabernet Sauvignon have been very successful, and Wallace wants to add the grape to his vineyard.

Making 15,000 gallons of wine a year, Hinzerling is a small winery with a keen interest in Washington's viticultural frontier.

THE HOGUE CELLARS

1982

Schwartzman Vineyards

Yakima Valley, Washington
WHITE RIESLING

Alcohol 11.5% by volume
PRODUCED AND BOTTLED BY THE HOGUE CELLARS, PROSSER, WA

The Hogue Cellars
(Roza Estates Winery)
Founded 1982
Route 2, Box 2898, Prosser, Washington 99350
(509) 786-4557

Monday through Saturday, 10 AM to 5 PM; Sunday, Noon to 5
PM; May through September. Call or write for winter hours.

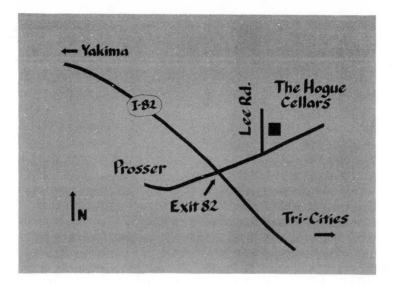

THE HOGUE CELLARS

The Hogue family, long established residents of the Yakima Valley, raise, among other things, hops, mint, cattle—and grapes. After several years as grape growers, the Hogues decided to open a winery of their own. Mike Conway, formerly winemaker at Worden's Washington Winery, a principal buyer of Hogue grapes, was hired as winemaker.

The same year that The Hogue Cellars started production, Conway opened a winery of his own in Spokane, commuting by private aircraft the 45 minute trip between his winery and the Hogue winery in the Yakima Valley. As Hogue's production increases, it will become less feasible for Conway to continue as winemaker, but the association will continue. Hogue will furnish grapes for Conway's Latah Creek Winery, and Conway will be retained as consultant to the Hogue winery.

Andy Markin, Hogue's assistant winemaker, tends to day to day winery operations. An agricultural economist, Markin wrote his Masters thesis on grape growing. His winery and viticultural activities, however, are only a portion of his varied duties for the diversified interests of Hogue Ranches.

The Yakima Valley is slightly cooler than most other growing climates in south-central Washington, and Riesling and Chenin Blanc, both delicate, floral/fruity grape varieties well suited to the cooler climate, make up a major portion of Hogue's production. To emphasize the delicate qualities of these grapes, alcohol content is targeted to between 10½ and 11½ percent. Although Hogue Rieslings are released with a high level of natural fruit acidity, they are not made in the same piquant style as typical German renderings of the grape, but are usually sweeter and richer, reflecting south-central Washington's ability and tendency to produce higher sugar levels in the fruit as well as good fruit acids.

When The Hogue Cellars reaches full production, the range of wines will include Riesling, Chenin Blanc, Chardonnay, Semillon, Sauvignon Blanc, Pinot Noir, Cabernet Sauvignon, and Merlot. The Cabernet Sauvignon will be blended with some Merlot. As Markin describes, although Cabernet Sauvignon is the nobler grape, displaying intense and complex varietal characteristics, its wine nevertheless seems often to have "hollow spots," as if the wine were not quite complete. The judicious addition of Merlot rounds out the Cabernet, adding texture and suppleness.

Most wineries, especially those that have substantial vineyards of their own, emphasize the importance of estate wines, wines made from the grapes of their own nearby vineyards. Although Hogue will certainly have most of the grapes to satisfy their production needs, Hogue's emphasis is not necessarily on estate wines.

The Hogues are committed to the local community of fellow ranchers, farmers, and grape growers. The winery is a natural local outlet for the grapes of nearby growers, and Hogue wants to emphasize this sense of community by purchasing other nearby Yakima grapes. The standard argument against purchased grapes is that the goals of the grower and winemaker are sometimes different, and the winemaker does not have the same intimate and final control as he does with his own grapes. These arguments are mitigated, however, in the instances where winemaker and grape grower develop a close working association, and a shared interest in the final product. Such an association and interest characterizes Hogue's relationship with local growers, and when the wines from individual vineyards merit special recognition, Hogue will identify the source on the label.

The Hogue Cellars soon will become one of the larger and more important winerys in the Yakima Valley. First year production was a modest 5,000 gallons, but the Hogue vineyards near Prosser and Sunnyside total nearly 200 acres, and when all their vines, and the vines of local growers, come into bearing, The Hogue Cellars will produce some 150,000 gallons a year.

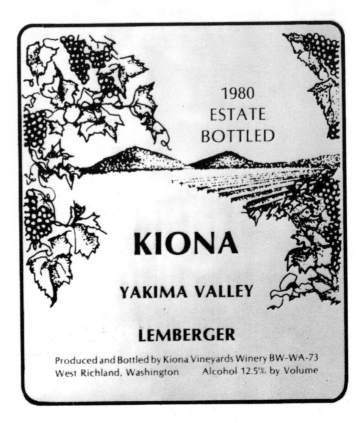

1980
ESTATE
BOTTLED

KIONA

YAKIMA VALLEY

LEMBERGER

Produced and Bottled by Kiona Vineyards Winery BW-WA-73
West Richland, Washington   Alcohol 12.5% by Volume

Kiona Vineyards
Founded 1979
Route 2, Box 2169E, Benton City, Washington 99320
(509) 967-3212

Daily, Noon to 5 PM, May through September.

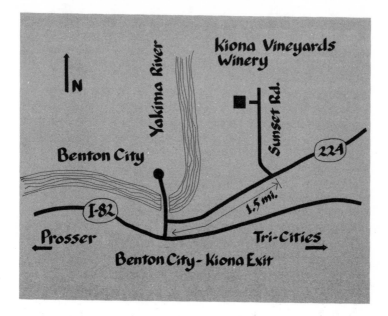

KIONA VINEYARDS

Kiona Vineyards is the partnership of two families, Jim and Pat Holmes, and John and Ann Williams. Since 1961, Holmes and Williams have worked together as engineers. Holmes, a native of San Francisco and long time home winemaker, describes the Kiona winery as a hobby that got out of hand. The idea for the venture began in 1973. In 1975, grapes were planted on the lower slopes of Red Mountain, near the town of Kiona, at the eastern end of the Yakima Valley.

The first grapes were sold to other wineries. In 1979, the Kiona Vineyards winery was bonded, and in 1980, the first commercial crush took place in the crowded but technically well equipped garage of the Holmes home.

Kiona Vineyards represents a growing trend toward "estate wineries." In the past, much of Washington's wine was produced in wineries far from the growing site, often from vineyards not under the direct control of the winemaker. The Williams home and new winery facility are located at the vineyard site, and nearly all of Kiona's grapes will come from their own vines.

Early in the growing season, John Williams shows the new clusters of Lemberger grapes.

The soil is a Hezel silt loam, running about 25 feet down to a 60 to 80 foot layer of sand and gravel. Unlike some vineyard sites in south-central Washington, the Kiona vineyard does not have a calcerous layer of hardpan near the soil's surface. Vineyard sites having this hardpan must be ripped and worked so that vine roots can penetrate far enough into the soil to be protected from winter cold.

Chenin Blanc and Riesling are the winery's staples. Kiona's Chardonnay, fermented half in French oak and half in stainless steel, is their premier white wine. A Cabernet Sauvignon, aged in American oak, completes what would be a typical range of wines marketed by a Washington winery.

But there is more. Kiona grows and produces Lemberger, a little known red wine grape with not much to recommend it in winegrowing traditions. Its most well-known viticultural roots are in Wurttemberg, Germany, a region not exactly known for exceptional red wines. From a commercial standpoint, it has no established market as does Riesling or Cabernet Sauvignon. Worse yet, the name is identified with a nasty smelling cheese. There is, it seems, little reason to bother with the grape—except that Washington State University professor emeritus Dr. Walter Clore was more interested

182

in performance on merit than in tradition or marketing. Dr. Clore has long recommended the grape for Washington's wine industry, and his recommendations have long been resisted for understandable, though regretable, reasons. Washington's wine industry is now established to the point that there is room for new ventures in exploration of Washington's unique growing climate. Recent interest in Lemberger is one example, and Kiona is one of the few wineries committed to the grape.

Commentary on Washington Lemberger can only be preliminary. In part because of the grape's flexibility, much more experience is needed to know the best style or styles for the grape. Lemberger can be successfully cropped higher than most red varieties. At Kiona, the vines are pruned for a yield of six tons an acre. Lemberger wines are typically deeply colored. The grape lends itself well to styles ranging from fruity, Beaujolais-like wines to more robust wines requiring lengthier aging. Even in the long-aging renditions, the wine retains good fruit and finesse. The ultimate importance of the grape will not be known for some time, but it is clear that Lemberger merits more attention.

Kiona has barely four acres of Lemberger. Many of the first plantings of delicate nursery stock were killed the first winter. These vines were replaced with more winter hardy rooted cuttings, and there have been no further problems with winter kill. Kiona's Lemberger is aged in American oak and made in a full bodied, tannic style, requiring bottle aging before it is at its best.

Kiona's total wine production is currently about 6,000 gallons a year, but as additional acreage is planted, and the younger vines in the 30 acre vineyard mature, wine production will increase substantially.

Franz Wilh. Langguth · *Wine since 1789*

1982
F. W. LANGGUTH[S]
LATE HARVEST
WHITE RIESLING

WASHINGTON STATE
From Selected Riesling grapes aged on the vines

ALCOHOL 9,5 %
BY VOLUME

750 ml

PRODUCED AND BOTTLED BY:
FRANZ WILHELM LANGGUTH WINERY BW-WA-87
MATTAWA, WASHINGTON 99344 .

F. W. Langguth Winery
Founded 1982
2340 S.W. Road F.5, Mattawa, Washington 99344
(509) 932-4943

Group tours only, by prior appointment.

F.W. LANGGUTH WINERY

The F. W. Langguth Winery is the first in the Northwest to be substantially financed by a foreign wine company, a trend now prevalent in the California wine industry. J. Wolfgang Langguth is the head of the family-owned German firm, F.W. Langguth Erben, GMBH, a huge winemaking operation headquartered at Traben-Trarbach in Germany's Mosel region.

In the late 70's, Langguth began looking around the world for a wine producing region to expand its operation. Such diverse areas as Brazil, North Africa, Australia, and California were considered, but on the advice of Dr. Helmut Becker, director of the famous German viticultural school at Geisenheim, Langguth chose Washington. Washington offered a climate suitable for growing Riesling and other German grape varieties, and local investment partners to participate in the venture.

The actual investment arrangement is rather complex, but essentially the German firm has majority interest in a Washington corporation which, in turn, is general partner in Washington's F.W. Langguth Winery. Langguth does not own any Washington vineyards per se, but has contracted long-term arrangements with a partnership called Weinbau, formed for the purpose of planting new vineyards in south-central Washington, on the Wahluke Slope near Mattawa. Seattle attorney, Alec Bayless, and retired folding-door manufacturer, Winslow Wright, two of the twelve principal partners in Sagemoor Farms, Washington's largest independent grape grower, are also general partners in Weinbau. The Langguths own one-third of the limited partnership interests in Weinbau.

The Weinbau vineyards, planted in 1981, consist of 221 acres. Sixty percent is in Riesling, 20 percent in Gewurztraminer, and 20 percent in Chardonnay. An additional 40 acres of Muscat Canelli and Riesling will be planted adjacent to the winery. No red varieties are planted, though Langguth produces some red wine from purchased grapes.

In Germany, though Riesling is by far the superior grape, growing conditions are marginal and much acreage is planted to lesser grapes, many of these vinifera crosses such as Muller-Thurgau, a genetic cross (though on this there is now some debate) of Riesling and Sylvaner. In the growing areas of south-central Washington, however, Riesling reliably produces relatively large

185

yields of good fruit, and there is not as much incentive to grow the lesser varieties. Langguth is emphasizing Riesling, but will experiment with small amounts of Muller-Thurgau and other grapes.

Max Zellweger is Langguth's winemaker. A graduate of the College of Technology, Viticulture, and Horticulture in Wadenswil, Switzerland, Zellweger was winemaker at Oregon's Chateau Benoit Winery before coming to Langguth. Zellweger's winemaking style emphasizes freshness and delicacy.

White wines are fermented in a temperature range of 45 to 55 degrees. Immediately after fermentation, the wines are centrifuged to remove all yeast cells. Prior to fermentation, the grape juice is also sometimes centrifuged to remove unwanted grape solids, a practice that contributes to a lighter, more delicate character. Langguth purchased state-of-the-art winemaking equipment for its new Washington winery, including an enclosed membrane press that allows juice yields of 165 to 170 gallons per ton without heavy pressing pressure, giving Langguth some of the best of both worlds, high yields and good quality juice.

Semi-dry wines can be made by stopping fermentation at the desired sweetness, or by completely fermenting the wine to dryness, then adding back unfermented grape juice to achieve the desired balance. Zellweger is experimenting with both methods to determine the best practice for his grapes.

The Langguth winery came onto the Northwest wine scene in a big way. Winemaking facilities were completed in August of 1982. The following month, Langguth began its first year's crush, 195,000 gallons. Langguth already has a 450,000 gallon tank capacity, and there are plans for future expansion.

While many Northwest wineries are just learning how to market wines outside the Northwest, Langguth's parent firm is a worldwide expert. F. W. Langguth's marketing department has been located in New York, far from winery's isolated setting in Mattawa. Washington's wine industry has long been in need of diversity. The many new, small wineries are augmenting one end of the spectrum. Langguth is doing its part at the larger end of the scale.

Washington State
JOHANNISBERG RIESLING

10.5% by volume
Produced and bottled by Washington Cellars
for Latah Creek Wine Cellars,
Spokane, Washington

Latah Creek Winery
Founded 1982
13030 East Indiana Avenue, Spokane, Washington 99216
(509) 448-0102 (temporary)

Monday through Saturday, 10 AM to 4 PM;
Sunday, Noon to 4 PM.

LATAH CREEK WINERY

For many years, Spokane, one of Washington's major metropolitan areas, has not participated in the state's wine boom. This is changing in the 1980's, and Latah Creek is one of the first in the growing trend of new wineries.

In 1980, Mike Conway, an experienced California winemaker, came to Washington to make wine for Worden's Washington Winery. After two years at Worden's, Conway left to start his own winery, Latah Creek. The same year, Conway became winemaker for Hogue Cellars in the Yakima Valley, commuting from Spokane by private aircraft. Conway will continue as Hogue's winemaker until Hogue's vineyards mature and Hogue grows large enough to require a full-time, on site winemaker. Formerly a grape supplier for Worden's, Hogue will be the major supplier for Latah Creek, as well as a financial partner. As Latah Creek becomes established, Conway will sever financial ties with Hogue, and he and his family will run the 40,000 gallon winery as a family business.

Unlike many new winemakers coming to Washington, Conway is a microbiologist, and not a winemaking graduate of U. C. Davis. While attending school, Conway worked nights as a lab technician for California's Gallo Winery. After graduating , he went to work for Franzia, and soon became directly interested in winemaking.

In 1977, Conway applied for an assistant winemaking position at Parcucci, not really expecting that they would hire someone without formal training in enology. At the time, however, Parducci was undergoing a massive expansion and needed someone who could insure the biological stability of their wines. Conway was hired, and became directly involved in the winemaking process.

One of Latah Creek's specialities is a direct result of his association with Parducci. Joe Monostori, Parducci's cellarmaster, learned winemaking in Hungary from his grandfather. In the spring, to celebrate the planting of new crops, the local Hungarian winemakers made May Wine, a light, sweet, fragrant wine flavored with woodruff and strawberries. At Parducci, Monostori made small quantities for sale only at the winery. Conway learned the recipe from Monostori, and May Wine has become a Latah Creek speciality, released each spring to coincide with Spokane's Lilac Festival.

Riesling and Chenin Blanc are Latah Creek's major wines. Both of these varietals are usually fermented slowly at cool temperatures to preserve their fresh fruity qualities. Different yeast strains behave differently. Some yeast strains "stick" at low temperatures and cannot be readily restarted, causing many problems for the winemaker. Conway, especially for his delicate white varietals, prefers the Steinberg strain. Steinberg ferments slowly and reliably at low temperatures, yet can be easily stopped when the desired sweetness is reached. Steinberg is expensive. Most of it comes in the form of liquid cultures from California, but Conway's is a dry culture from Germany that he obtains from Canada via the barter system, trading some of his grape juice for the yeast.

Sometimes chemical preservatives called sorbates are added to semi-sweet wines to insure their stability, and prevent refermentation in the bottle and other such maladies. Sorbates, however, if used to any great degree, adversely affect the flavor of the wine. Because of Conway's training in microbiology, Parducci, for the first time, was able to completely eliminate sorbates in most of their wines. At Latah Creek, Conway is again employing his skills in microbiology to avoid chemical preservatives.

Conway likes to keep his delicate white wines cool from the onset of fermentation through the bottling process. Keeping the wine continuously cool traps carbon dioxide and makes the wine slightly "spritzy" when the bottle is opened and the wine is served. The slight effervescence from the release of the trapped gas contributes to the wine's fresh taste.

Conway has definite ideas about the kind of wine he wants to make. In his view, some wineries rely on one or two speciality wines to win medals in competitions, and then raise the price of their other wines that have gained prestige by association. Taking a cue from Parducci, a winery that has long had a reputation for good wine at a reasonable price, Conway is not emphasizing expensive speciality wines, but good wines at modest prices.

Mont Elise Vineyards
(Bingen Wine Cellars)

Founded 1974

P. O. Box 28, (315 West Steuben), Bingen, Washington 98605
(509) 493-3001

Thursday through Saturday, Noon to 4:30 PM.

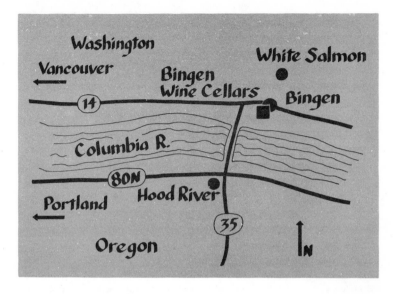

MONT ELISE VINEYARDS

The first Bingen wines were marketed under the name Bingen Wine Cellars, but in late 1978, the Charles Henderson family bought out the other winery partners and became sole owners, changing the winery's primary name to Mont Elise Vineyards.

Charles Henderson has been involved with agronomy all his life, and for the past 15 years, has been growing grapes in the Bingen area. During this time, he has worked closely with Dr. Clore and others from the Irrigated Agricultural Research and Extension Center at Prosser, Washington to evaluate the grape varieties best suited to the Bingen area.

From about 20 experimentally planted grape varieties, Pinot Noir and Gewurztraminer were selected as the best, and in 1972, Henderson planted his vineyards to them. Eighteen acres are now bearing, and there are plans to expand to an eventual 40 acres. Henderson is considering other varieties, but will ultimately produce no more than four, believing that quality usually suffers when a small winery attempts to make more than four different wines.

The Cascade Mountains and the Columbia River Gorge are remarkable geologic phenomena, and their climatic influence is no less profound. The Mont Elise vineyards are just east of where the

Columbia River Gorge cuts through the line of the Cascade Range. The Cascades block the easterly flow of marine air, making much of eastern Washington a desert while leaving western Washington moist, temperate, and lushly vegetated. The Columbia River Gorge is a passageway allowing the two dramatically different climates to interface. Understandably, radical climatic changes occur within relatively few miles, and parts of the gorge are characterized by this tempestuous mixing of climates.

In terms of the commonly used heat summation method of climate measurement, heat units at Mont Elise's vineyards range from 2,000 to 2,100 a year. A short distance west, and heat units measure 1,800 or less; a short distance east, and heat units measure 2,900 or higher. Thus, the microclimate is very tightly defined, probably the most highly localized microclimate of any grape growing area in the Northwest.

Microclimates, however, are much more complex than the measure of relative heat units. Henderson points out that Mont Elise receives slightly fewer heat units than growing areas in Oregon's Willamette Valley, yet Mont Elise grapes generally harvest one to two Brix higher in any given year. And although the little Cabernet Sauvignon that is planted in the northern Willamette Valley is high acid and does not ripen easily, Mont Elise's experimental Cabernet Sauvignon plantings ripen very well, yet are acid deficient. Heat unit measurements are good viticultural indicators, but it is increasingly apparent that supplementary measurement systems are needed, particularly in the Northwest.

Henderson makes a Chenin Blanc from grapes grown at the Don Graves Vineyard, 17 miles east of Bingen. Situated on a peninsula jutting into the Columbia River, the Graves Vineyard is itself a narrowly defined microclimate. Receiving about 2,900 heat units a year, the vineyard is subject to cool autumn winds moving through the gorge, ripening the grapes much differently than if they were grown in a warm stagnant climate.

Oregon oak *(Quercus garryana)* has recently received considerable attention. Not only is the wood readily available and much less expensive than French oaks, but blind taste tests indicate its flavor is quite similar to those found in French oaks, and there is now the prospect of using native Northwest oak with Northwest wines.

Henderson was one of the first to begin working with the Oregon oak, but a shortage of even small quantities of cured oak delayed early efforts. Henderson intends to make the oak barrels

The Mont Elise winery in Bingen.

himself from trees growing on his property. Because there is some question about the bendability of the oak, Henderson's first barrels will actually be small 200 to 400 gallon tanks.

From early experiments, Dr. Clore and others believed Pinot Noir the most promising variety for the Bingen microclimate, and Henderson has chosen to center his efforts on this most difficult grape. Early efforts were encouraging, but beginning in 1978, the Pinot Noirs were put through a malolactic fermentation, and the improvement in these later wines was remarkable.

Most winemakers believe Pinot Noir requires relatively high fermentation temperatures to achieve good color and varietal character. Henderson is no exception, fermenting his Pinot Noir in the low to mid 90's, a temperature even higher than most other winemakers of the high temperature school. At a about a decade old, Henderson feels his Pinot Noir vines are just getting into their prime for producing distinctive wines.

Bingen crushes 10,000 gallons annually, but there are plans for expansion, and Henderson's son, Charles Jr., is studying enology at the University of California at Davis, and will be returning as a partner in the operation.

Mount Baker Vineyards

Founded 1982
4298 Mount Baker Highway, Everson, Washington 98247
(206) 592-2300

Wednesday through Sunday, 11 AM to 6 PM.

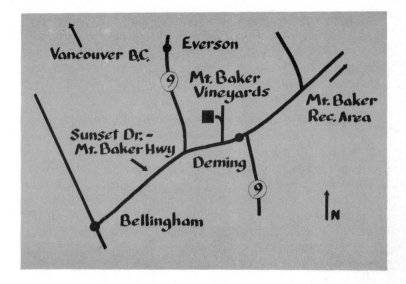

MOUNT BAKER VINEYARDS

Washington has two distinct climates. West of the Cascade Mountain Range is a marine climate, characterized by cool summers, moderate winters, and frequent clouds and rain. East of the Cascades, the climate is cooler in the winter and much warmer in the summer. The skies are frequently cloudless, and there is little rain.

Although the first premium grape wineries in the modern era were located in metropolitan areas west of the Cascades, virtually all the grapes were grown east of the Cascades in the south-central portion of the state. South-central Washington will undoubtedly always remain the state's biggest winegrowing region, but there is now keen interest in growing wine grapes west of the Cascades.

Al Stratton, founder of Mount Baker Vineyards, and Jim Hildt, horticulturist and partner in the winery, are major proponents of western Washington winegrowing. A retired military physician, Stratton became involved with research projects at Washington State University's Research and Extension Unit at Mount Vernon, Washington. When the time came to make wine from the experimentally grown grapes, the research center's horticulturist, Bob Norton, turned to Stratton. The Mt. Vernon area, averaging less than 1,600 heat units during the growing season, is far from the best grape growing climate in western Washington, but Stratton was impressed that good quality wine could be made even in this very cool area.

Many areas west of the Cascades are far better suited to growing grapes. The site of Stratton's own vineyards is in one such area. The vineyard is located 11½ miles east of Bellingham, Washington in a microclimate a quarter mile wide and two miles long. Even though the vineyards are on the valley floor, nighttime thermal air currents keep the vines frost free during the growing season, a season that lasts from 210 to 240 days, longer than the growing season in most south-central Washington vineyards. Stratton recorded approximately 2,100 heat units for two recent successive years, neither of which were particularly warm. Although heat unit measurements by no means tell the whole story, they are important indicators, and Stratton's measurements bode well for the success of the area.

The grapes that do well in western Washington are, for the most part, different than those that do well in south-central Washington. Madeleine Angevine and Okanagan Riesling are Stratton's major grape varieties. Madeleine Angevine is a Semillon-like vinifera variety. Okanagan Riesling, a grape brought to the New World by Hungarian immigrants, and named after a Canadian Valley, is a variety of mysterious origin. Canadian viticulturists now believe that it is not actually a vinifera variety, but a hybrid. It is, nevertheless, considered a good quality wine grape. Stratton is also working with another hybrid, Leon Millot, a cool climate red variety similar, but perhaps superior, to Marechal Foch. The major emphasis, however, is on the vinifera varieties. These include Madeleine Angevine, Madeleine Sylvaner, Gewurztraminer, Pinot Noir, Muller-Thurgau, and Chardonnay. The Geisenheim Institute in Germany actively develops new vinifera crosses for cool climate growing environments. As more of these become available in Washington, Stratton will plant them in his vineyard.

In 1982, the first year of Mount Baker's existence, Stratton crushed 13,000 gallons from western Washington grapes. Future production from wine grapes is expected to reach 20,000 gallons. Stratton uses neither grapes nor grape juice from outside western Washington, a claim that few others can make. Stratton's own 20

Al Stratton and Jim Hildt, tying dormant canes after pruning.

acre vineyard is the source of most of his grapes. Others nearby are also planting vineyards.

Like Oregon, and unlike California and south-central Washington, Mount Baker's vines are cane pruned rather than cordon pruned, a more involved pruning method common in much of Europe, and more suitable to cooler climates. More than 900 vines are planted per acre, a moderately dense spacing, typical of cool climate viticultural practices, designed to reduce the burden on each vine. Soil is important. Most of Stratton's vineyard is a sandy alluvial soil, but a very small section is heavier and more clay-like. The vines planted in this section are more prone to excess vegetative growth, and the grapes do not ripen as easily.

Of the more familiar grape varieties, Stratton believes that Pinot Noir will make a flavorful rose in cool years, and a Burgundian-style red wine in warmer years. Stratton is particularly enthused about the prospects of Chardonnay. In the western United States, except for pest resistance, there is little interest in specialized rootstocks, but growers in Europe's cooler climates work extensively with different rootstocks in conjunction with various grape varieties to bring out the best in the vine according to soil type and climatic conditions. Stratton is experimenting with different rootstocks for his Chardonnay, a variety he feels will benefit considerably from rootstock selection.

Stratton's experimentation extends beyond winegrowing. Four species of oak are used at the Mount Baker winery. Some wineries flavor their wines with oak chips as an expedient, either because the experimental wood they wish to test has not cured long enough to cooper into barrels, or is not physically suitable to cooper into barrels, or, more often, simply to avoid purchasing the expensive barrels.

Stratton's perspective is different. In his opinion, red wines may benefit from the controlled oxidation that takes place in wood barrels, but white wines suffer from such treatment. Stratton prefers to keep white wines in stainless steel, adding oak chips to the tank if oak character is desired. He goes further in his assessment of oaks, suggesting that the denser harder heartwood is preferable for red wine while the softer sapwood is milder, marrying best with white wine. More than two decades ago, Stratton planted several European oak species on his property. The trees have matured enough to thin, and can now provide an abundant source of oak chips for the winery. Stratton believes that some of the oaks that are not suitable for coopering into barrels could prove superior in flavor to traditional oaks.

Western Washington wine is the orphan of the state's wine industry. Nearly all the state's research funds for winegrowing are directed east of the Cascades, to Washington's agri-business heartland. Stratton describes Mount Baker Vineyards as research oriented, a good thing, since only minimal research support is available from the state. At this stage of western Washington winegrowing, combining research with a commercial enterprise is almost a necessity, and Mount Baker Vineyards is well equipped for the task.

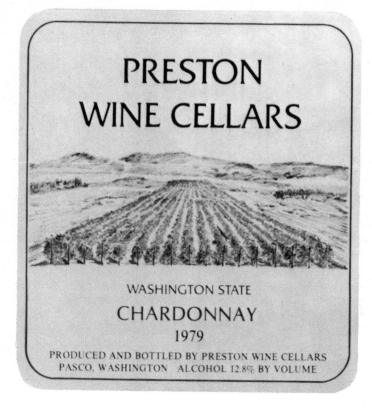

PRESTON
WINE CELLARS

WASHINGTON STATE
CHARDONNAY
1979

PRODUCED AND BOTTLED BY PRESTON WINE CELLARS
PASCO, WASHINGTON   ALCOHOL 12.8% BY VOLUME

Preston Wine Cellars

Founded 1976
Star Route 1, Box 1234, Pasco, Washington 99301
(509) 545-1990

Daily, 10 AM to 5:30 PM, except major holidays.

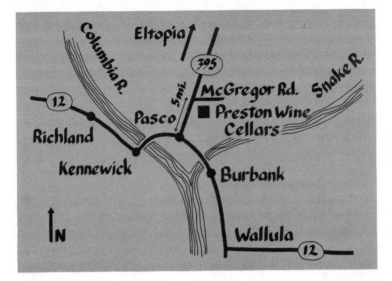

PRESTON WINE CELLARS

Preston Wine Cellars is located in the Columbia Basin of eastern Washington, five miles north of Pasco on Highway 395. A large 48 foot sign marks the entrance to the winery estate. An estate in the true sense, the winery is on property contiguous with the Preston family home. The vineyards surround the winery and extend into the distance.

To those accustomed to the dramatic grandeur of lushly green mountains and snowcapped peaks, the Columbia Basin looks stark, empty, and desolate. But this desert of flatlands and rolling hills commands its own grandeur by its very vastness. And then too, it can be argued that in the lushly green areas of the Northwest, one is so continuously bombarded with so much stimuli that nothing really stands out, nothing is really seen. In the Columbia Basin, every sensory happening stands forth and commands attention. Some have remarked that its furrowed fields are like a Zen garden on a vast scale.

But Bill Preston's cultural base is that of a self-made man in the American tradition. A native of the area, he and his family are the owners and operators of Preston Wine Cellars, the Northwest's

Ready for the hectic harvest.

largest family-owned winery. Established in 1976, yearly production is now 120,000 gallons, and future capacity may reach the
250,000 gallon mark. Robert Griffin is the winemaker.

The vineyard estate is planted to 11 varieties: Chardonnay,
Riesling, Cabernet Sauvignon, Pinot Noir, Sauvignon Blanc,
Chenin Blanc, Gewurztraminer, Merlot, Gamay Beaujolais, Muscat
of Alexandria, and Royalty. The vineyard consists of 181 acres.
The first fifty acres were planted in 1972 and 1973, the remainder
planted in 1979.

It is generally thought, and usually rightly so, that the very
best wines are produced by small wineries concentrating intense
personal attention on small quantities of two or three wines. But
there are notable exceptions, or at least variances from the general
rule. Sensitive to questions concerning a winery's ability to achieve
excellence while producing large quantities of a wide variety of
wines, Preston cites the reputation of California's Robert Mondavi
Winery, producing often outstanding wine in much greater quantities than even the maximum projected for Preston Wine Cellars.
Preston believes much of the problem with large premium wineries
lies in their control by parent corporations that are completely
oriented to the immediate cost effectiveness of every winemaking
step. The quality decline in a number of premium California wineries
purchased by large corporations seems to support Preston's view.
If there is the desire to produce fine wines, and the necessary

After the grapes are crushed, the stems are hauled away for disposal.

money, equipment, skills, dedication, and freedom to do so, Preston believes there is no reason larger wineries cannot produce the very finest wines.

The Columbia Basin is one of the warmest growing areas in Washington. As might be expected, Preston is convinced that this area produces the finest wines in the Northwest, and moreover, is one of the world's best viticultural regions. Preston characterizes the area as a huge natural greenhouse. The desert soil is too dry and sandy to support much natural vegetation, yet it is a viticultural medium that is highly receptive to the means and ends of winegrowing technology. Precise moisture control is achieved through irrigation; desired nutrient balance is maintained by adding fertilizers to the neutral sandy soil; and the warm sunny climate means there is little chance rain will fall at inopportune times.

The climate is well suited to many important grape varieties, and individual sections of Preston's vineyard can be cooled by a computerized sprinkler system. *Botrytis cinerea*, the mold responsible for special sweet wines, is naturally occurring, and can be encouraged when desirable, and prevented when not. Vineyard yield can be restricted for varietal intensity, or increased to levels rivaling California's Central Valley while maintaining adequate sugar-acid balance and varietal profile. The Columbia Basin is the Northwest's most versatile winegrowing region.

This is not to say the area is without problems. A good portion of Preston's first plantings was destroyed the following winter. The cold is a problem most winters, and the 1978-1979 winter inflicted considerable damage on Preston's vines, particularly Cabernet Sauvignon and Sauvignon Blanc. More recently planted vines were rooted deeper into the soil to protect the roots from drying and freezing. And although a weedy vineyard looks less attractive than one carefully manicured, Preston has found that a groundcover of weeds helps protect the vines in winter.

The Preston tasting room is directly over the winery, and large windows and an open deck provide a panoramic view of the vineyard estate and surrounding countryside. The facility has seating for 60 visitors, and a gift shop where wine related items can be purchased. Some of Preston's speciality wines such as botrytised Riesling and Sauvignon Blanc are available only at the tasting room. For those interested in the workings of a winery, there is a self-guided tour.

Preston wines are marketed in Washington, Idaho, Oregon, and California. Expansion to select national markets is expected soon.

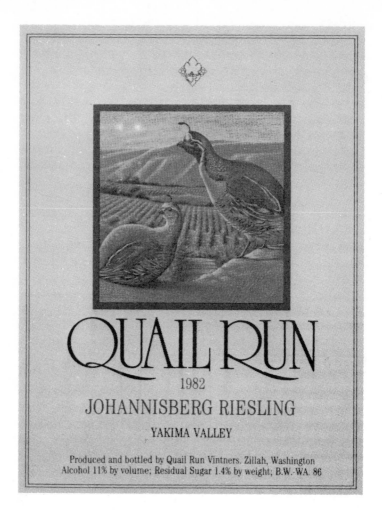

1982

JOHANNISBERG RIESLING

YAKIMA VALLEY

Produced and bottled by Quail Run Vintners, Zillah, Washington
Alcohol 11% by volume; Residual Sugar 1.4% by weight; B.W. WA. 86

Quail Run Vintners
Founded 1982
Route 2, Box 2287, Zillah, Washington 98953
(509) 829-6235

Monday through Saturday, 10 AM to 5 PM; spring through fall, also open Sunday, Noon to 5 PM. Group tours by appointment.

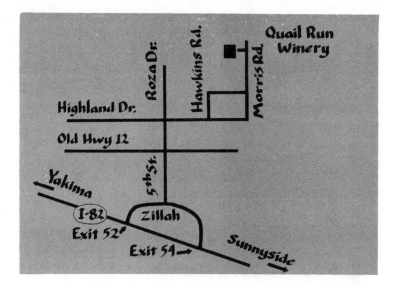

QUAIL RUN VINTNERS

The Yakima Valley is one of Washington's most important viticultural regions. Generally cooler than the other major growing areas in south-central Washington, the Yakima Valley is smaller and relatively more populated than the vast openness of growing sites in other parts of the Columbia Basin. Washington's larger wineries have traditionally developed their vineyards outside the Yakima Valley. Quail Run is the first winery of substantial size to make wine solely from Yakima grapes.

In 1982, their first crush, Quail Run made 33,000 gallons of wine. As the vineyards mature, and if the wine market is favorable, Quail Run will eventually produce 125,000 gallons annually, not a huge production, but considerably out of the boutique category. Eighty-five percent of Quail Run's wine is white, the majority, Riesling.

Stan Clarke heads the partnership of twenty owners. Clarke graduated from U.C. Davis with a degree in viticulture, and worked for several California vineyards and Washington's Chateau Ste. Michelle before coming to Quail Run. Clarke is marketing director as well as viticulturist and vineyard manager. The two Quail Run

The newly completed Quail Run winery.

vineyards are owned separately by two of the winery's partners, and the grapes are sold to the Quail Run partnership. Together, the vineyards total 175 acres.

The winery and one of the vineyards is in an area near Zillah called Whiskey Canyon. It is an orchard area, and spring frosts have not been a problem. The soil is a Burke sandy loam. It is an excellent vineyard soil, but because it is more claylike than other soils in the area, it is not, in Clarke's opinion, ideal for varietals like Sauvignon Blanc and Chenin Blanc. Both these varietals have high vine vigor, and the extra moisture retained by the clay in the soil would make the vines difficult to control and crop properly. Neither varietal is grown on this site.

Quail Run's vineyards were planted in 1980. The vines are planted six feet apart within the rows with a ten foot spacing between each row. California vineyards are planted with as much as ten feet between the vines and twelve feet between the rows. Some Washington vineyards are planted to this wider spacing, but Clarke prefers a closer spacing so that less demand is put on the individual root systems. Chardonnay and Cabernet Sauvignon are cropped to a yield of 4½ tons an acre, Riesling to 6 tons an acre.

A graduate in enology from U. C. Davis, Wayne Marcil, Quail Run's winemaker, was winemaker at California's Monterey Peninsula Winery before coming to the Northwest. It is Marcil's winemaking philosophy to show off the inherent crispness and natural acidity of Yakima Valley wines. Riesling and Gewurztraminer are fermented at a temperature of 50 degrees, Chardonnay at 55 degrees. Quail Run's Chardonnays have not needed malolactic fermentation or any other method of acid reduction. Marcil feels that any of these methods are detrimental to Chardonnay.

Quail Run makes wine from two less common grape varieties, Morio Muscat, a high yielding genetic cross of Sylvaner and Pinot Blanc, and Lemberger, a red wine grape grown in Wurttemberg, Germany. Quail Run was the first Northwest winery to release Morio Muscat as an individual varietal bottling. Lemberger is a little known, but promising, Washington grape variety. It can be made in a tannic, oaky style, needing bottle aging before it is consumed, or as a fresh, fruity, quaffing wine. Quail Run makes the latter style, and slightly chilled, considers it an ideal summer red wine.

Not without good reason, Yakima Valley winegrowers consider their area one of Washington's most important premium winegrowing regions. Clarke wants Quail Run to be the showcase for the Yakima Valley, and Quail Run's tasting room and visitor facilities were an important and integral part of the winery's design.

Paul Thomas Wines
Founded 1979
1717 136th Place N.E., Bellevue, Washington 98005
(206) 747-1008

Tasting and tours by appointment only. Group tours and one week's advanced notice are preferred. Case sales are available.

PAUL THOMAS WINES

On a wall in the Paul Thomas winery, in elegant calligraphy, is a poster with a quote by John Stuart Mill from "On Liberty." The quote reads, "Eccentricity has always abounded when and where strength of character has abounded. And the amount of eccentricity in a society has generally been proportional to the amount of genius, mental vigor, and moral courage it contained. That too few dare to be eccentric marks the chief danger of our time."

The quotation is no less than a rallying cry for Paul Thomas, a vinous call to arms. Something of a dichotomy has evolved, wherein serious wine drinkers always drink vinifera grape wines, and these wines are almost always dry. Non-serious wine drinkers drink fruit and berry wines, and these are always sweet. Paul Thomas wines militate against this dichotomy. With one exception, all Paul Thomas fruit wines are dry—wines for the table, wines meant to accompany food, wines, in Paul Thomas's view, for the serious wine drinker.

Thomas makes table wines from vinifera grape wines as well as from fruit. Although most makers of premium grape wines would not think of defiling their product line with fruit wines, Thomas sees no inconsistency in his combined approach.

He believes, in fact, that his approach is more in line with the basic concept of "premium table wine" than many who make only grape wines. Most grape wineries rely on sweet or semi-sweet wines for a major portion of their production. Paul Thomas does not. Whether fruit wine or grape wine, most of Thomas's wines are dry.

Crimson Rhubarb accounts for seventy percent of the winery's production. Although it has some residual sugar, the taste is quite dry, and the wine goes well with food. Crimson Rhubarb has a light pinkish blush, and the appearance and taste is somewhat reminiscent of a white wine made from red grapes, such as white Zinfandel or Pinot Noir Blanc. It has done well against these wines in competitions.

Most wineries make Riesling with considerable residual sweetness for the broadest popular appeal. Thomas's White Riesling has fairly high acid and less than one percent residual sugar. He has been told that if he increased the residual sugar to about two percent he could sell five times as much wine, but Thomas

Paul Thomas.

is cutting back production instead, and continuing to make the wine in a less sweet style, a style consistent with his approach.

Paul Thomas became interested in wine on a trip to Paris in 1960, and has been studying and drinking wine ever since. He began making vinifera grape wine at home in 1968. A Wenatchee native, some of his friends from the area suggested he make wine from Bing cherries, and so began his interest in dry table wines made from fruits. When the time came to open a commercial winery, in 1979, Thomas decided it would be better to enter the market with a unique product, dry fruit wines, rather than trying to improve on and compete with the vinifera grape wines already on the market. The popularity of Crimson Rhubarb has proven the success of his thesis—and there has been little competition.

Raspberry is Paul Thomas's only truly sweet wine, and his only berry wine. Made in small quantities from organically grown raspberries, it has become a traditional release for the holidays. As Thomas explains, berries do not make good dry wines. Because berries are high in acid and low in sugar, their juice must be either be diluted with water, or sweetened, or both. Non-berry fruit wines, however, do have the appropriate balance of sugar and acid to make good dry wines, and these are the focus of Thomas's efforts. The "fruit" wines include Dry Bartlett Pear, Crimson Rhubarb, and Elegance, a wine made from Bing cherries. Apricot and nectarine are also made as time and production facilities permit.

Thomas takes exception to the belief that fruit wines do not benefit from aging. Some do not. Crimson Rhubarb is best fresh, within six to nine months of fermentation, and Dry Bartlett Pear is best within eighteen months after release, but some do age much longer. Thomas's Dry Bing Cherry is a case in point. The wine itself is somewhat similar to a red grape wine. Although there are subdued cherry flavors, the wine does not taste strongly of fresh cherries, just as most grape wines do not have the taste of fresh grapes. Some have characterized the wine as reminiscent of Pinot Noir, a description that is not quite as farfetched as it first sounds. Thomas indicates that his 1979 Dry Bing Cherry is not only holding up well, but continues to improve in the bottle. Since there is little information on the aging of fruit wines, evaluation of their long term potential awaits the future.

Federal regulations prohibit vintage dating of fruit wines, but the lot numbers on Paul Thomas wines tell the story. Lot 783, for example, means that the fruit was crushed and fermented in July of 1983.

Paul Thomas produces about 6,000 gallons of grape wine a year, including Cabernet Sauvignon, Sauvignon Blanc, White Riesling, and Muscat Canelli. Total wine production is about 40,000 gallons a year. Thomas had expected that half of his production would be in grape wines by now, but because of the difficult wine market, Thomas continues to rely on his "speciality" dry fruit wines to carve out a marketing niche. It is his eventual goal to expand to about 160,000 gallons a year, relocate the winery east of the Cascades, and grow Pinot Noir on the shores of lake Chelan.

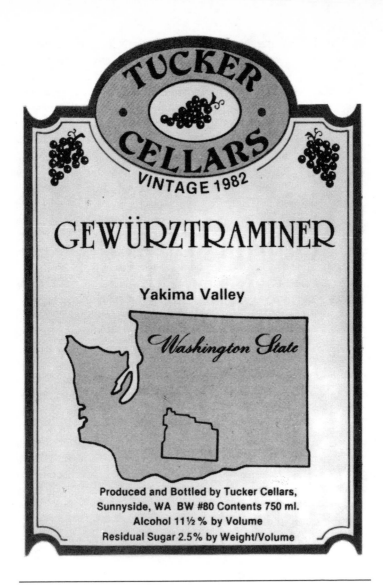

TUCKER CELLARS

VINTAGE 1982

GEWÜRZTRAMINER

Yakima Valley

Washington State

Produced and Bottled by Tucker Cellars,
Sunnyside, WA BW #80 Contents 750 ml.
Alcohol 11½ % by Volume
Residual Sugar 2.5% by Weight/Volume

Tucker Cellars
Founded 1981
Route 1, Box 1696, Sunnyside, Washington 98944
(509) 837-8701

Summer months, daily, 9 AM to 7 PM;
winter months, daily, 11 AM to 4 PM.

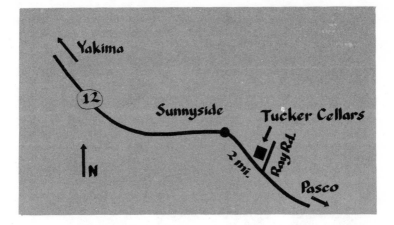

TUCKER CELLARS

Tucker Cellars may be one of Washington's newer wineries, but Dean Tucker's heritage goes to the very roots of Washington's vinifera wine industry. Born in 1930, Tucker has lived all his life in the Yakima Valley, near the community of Sunnyside.

Washington's first vinifera grape winery, the Upland Winery at Sunnyside, was founded in 1936, shortly after repeal of prohibition, by W.B. Bridgman. Dean Tucker's father was one of the original growers supplying grapes to supplement Bridgman's own plantings, and Tucker remembers working in his father's vineyard as a child. The Tucker family's first vineyard included Malvoisie, Muscat, Riesling, and Semillon grapes.

In his book, The Wines of America, wine authority Leon Adams reports tasting some of the Upland wines in the 1940s and finding them not particularly well made. Washington's first vinifera winery ceased operations after only a short existence. With little market for the grapes, the Tuckers moved off their vineyard property, and shortly thereafter, the vineyards were pulled up, and the land was planted to sugar beets.

Tucker has seen crops come and go as interest and needs wax and wane. After sugar beets, came orchards, then grapes and row crops, then sugar beets again. And in 1980, on 22 acres of the Tucker family's 500 acre farm, wine grapes were again planted.

Dean Tucker.

The plantings of Riesling, Chenin Blanc, Gewurztraminer, and Chardonnay will be increased eight to ten acres each year.

The Tucker farm is very much a family business. All of Tucker's four children are involved in the operation. The farm includes a 40 acre orchard, hay, and a variety of row crops. The winery building itself is an extension of the Tucker fruit and vegetable stand. This diversification provides a steady year-round work cycle for the Tucker family and their employees. After the apples are picked, the grapes are ready for harvest and crush. Late fall and winter allow time for work in the winery.

In the first year of operation, Tucker produced only Riesling and Chenin Blanc, both white wines, neither requiring aging in small oak barrels. For a winery just beginning operation, avoiding the use of oak means a considerable savings in money and labor, but in no way can operation costs be considered cheap. Each of Tucker's 1,600 gallon tanks cost $6,000. The tanks feature a movable top so that air space can be reduced according to the quantity of wine in the tank. Like most tanks designed for fermentation of delicate white grape varieties, coolant can be pumped through stainless steel "jackets" surrounding each tank to keep fermentation temperatures at about 50 degrees. If the must (juice from the grapes) were left to ferment on its own in large tanks, the heat generated by fermentation would raise temperatures enough to destroy delicate flavors.

Since the first crush, Chardonnay, Gewurztraminer, and Cabernet Sauvignon have been added, along with French and American oak barrels. The first year, Tucker produced 3,500 gallons of wine. Seven thousand gallons were made the following year. Tucker expects to double production each year until the winery's 50,000 gallon capacity is reached.

1982

WASHINGTON STATE

Chardonnay

PRODUCED & BOTTLED BY WORDEN'S WASHINGTON WINERY
SPOKANE, WA   BW WA 75   ALCOHOL 13.0% BY VOLUME

Worden's Washington Winery
Founded 1980
7217 West 45th, Spokane, Washington 99204
(509) 455-7835

Monday through Friday, 10 AM to 4 PM;
Saturday, 10 AM to 5 PM; Sunday, Noon to 5 PM.

WORDEN'S WASHINGTON WINERY

A native of central Washington, Jack Worden was looking to expand his apple orchards when he got caught up in the enthusiasm of Washington's wine boom. A transition from growing apples to growing grapes seemed like the logical course of action, but when learning that Washington had more than ample vineyard acreage but too few wineries, Worden set aside the idea of grape growing to open Spokane's first commercial winery in the modern era. Worden did not enter into the wine business without thought or preparation. He attended Washington seminars, and short courses on the economics of winery operations from the University of California at Davis.

Worden's winemaker, Rollin Soles, comes from an eclectic winemaking background. A graduate of U.C. Davis, Soles worked at California's Chateau Montelena for a year, for a year in Burgundy and Bordeaux, and in Australia for another year with an enological consulting team.

Ninety percent of Worden's grapes come from the 80 acre Moreman Vineyard near Pasco. The Moreman grapes display a distinctive style, and have shown well in comparison with grapes from other growers in the area. The vineyard's Sauvignon Blanc has been particularly good. Worden's long-term arrangement with Moreman allows the winery to maintain a distinctive and consistent style, an option not available to wineries that buy grapes from one grower one year and another grower the next.

Worden produces very little red wine. Consumer demand ultimately dictates what wines will be made, and America is currently in the middle of a tremendous white wine boom. Moreover, because those new to wine prefer slightly sweet wines, there is less demand, and therefore less production of the "dry" white varietals, Chardonnay and Sauvignon Blanc. Nearly a half of Worden's production is in Riesling, a wine usually made with some residual sugar.

Cabernet Sauvignon, Worden's only red wine, is aged in American oak. Worden's first Chardonnay was also aged in American oak, but since 1982, both the Chardonnay and Fume Blanc (Sauvignon Blanc) have had the benefit of small French oak barrels.

221

When conditions are right, special late harvest dessert wines are made. Riesling and Gewurztraminer are the major varieties for these rich sweet wines. The grapes for late harvest wines are sometimes not picked for two months or more after the regular harvest. Worden's late harvest wines, produced in small quantities, are sometimes available only at the winery.

Worden produces 25,000 gallons of wine a year. Expansion will continue until the winery's 50,000 gallon capacity is reached. A long time fruit grower, Jack Worden is still considering a vineyard of his own, a decision that will be made in the next few years as the variables of grape supply, wine production, and consumer demand sort themselves out.

VINTAGE 1980

Yakima River Winery

Yakima Valley

MERLOT

CEIL DU CHEVAL VINEYARD

Produced and Bottled by Yakima River Winery
Prosser, Wash. B.W.71 Alcohol 12% by Volume

Yakima River Winery
Founded 1978
Route 1, Box 1657, North River Road, Prosser, Washington 99350
(509) 786-2805

Daily, 10 AM to 5 PM, but call ahead to make sure someone is at the winery.

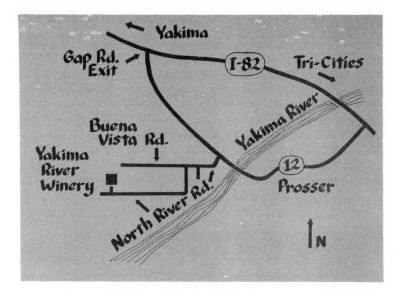

YAKIMA RIVER WINERY

Most Washington winemakers are lifelong residents of the state. Not so for John and Louise Rauner, who moved to Washington from New York for the specific purpose of making Washington wine. On a vacation trip through Washington in 1974, the Rauners purchased a few grapes and made two gallons of wine in their travel trailer. John Rauner had been making homemade wine since the late 1960's, but even under the primitive conditions of the travel trailer, the wine was far superior to what he had made in New York. The following year, the Rauners moved to the Yakima Valley. To prepare for what would become his new trade, Rauner took chemistry and other related classes, attended short courses at the University of California at Davis, and studied winemaking texts.

Unlike most Washington wineries located on the east side of the Cascades, the Yakima River Winery, with only three acres of vines, relies almost totally on grapes purchased from independent growers. There are pros and cons to being a winemaker only, and not a winegrower. From his perspective, Rauner feels he could not do justice to both grape growing and winemaking—both highly demanding and time consuming activities. Nearly all of Yakima River's grapes come from the Yakima Valley, and most come from smaller vineyards. Rauner develops a close working relationship with the growers, and provides additional quality incentives by often displaying vineyard names on Yakima River's labels. Rauner feels that he can select the best available grapes. If he were to have his own vineyard, he would be committed to using those grapes whether or not his vineyard site proved good or bad.

Many of Yakima River's grapes come from the Ceil du Cheval Vineyard at the far eastern end of the Valley. Planted on the lower slopes of Red Mountain, the vineyard has been completely free of spring frost. Though cooler than much of the Columbia Basin to the east, the vineyards are among the warmest in the Yakima Valley.

Producing wine since 1979, the Yakima River Winery came fully into its own with the 1981 vintage. In that year, temperature controlled fermentation tanks were available for fermenting Riesling, Chenin Blanc, and Gewurztraminer, wines that usually show their best when fermented at very cool temperatures. Because grape ripening and adequate sugar levels are rarely a problem in the growing areas of south-central Washington, there is sometimes the temptation, or necessity, to make wines higher in alcohol. Rauner strives for a moderate 11 percent alcohol in his delicate white varieties, a practice, that along with cool fermentation temperatures, preserves the delicate fruit flavors of these wines.

Chardonnay is fermented in French oak barrels, a practice that often benefits the grape. Somewhat unusually, Rauner's Merlot is also partially fermented in oak barrels. The fermentation is begun in stainless steel tanks, then at about 8 degrees Brix, the must is taken off the skins and pulp, and fermentation is completed in small American oak barrels. Both the Chardonnay and Merlot come from the Ciel du Cheval Vineyard. Washington red wines sometimes have a higher pH than desireable, but Rauner reports that the grapes he purchases yield Merlots with lower pH, typically around 3.2.

Gewurztraminer is Yakima River's speciality. It is a difficult wine to make well. With most varieties, the emphasis is on picking the grapes at a certain sugar level. Gewurztraminer, on the other hand, is often picked with more attention to acid than sugar. If the variety is picked too late, and the acids drop too much, the grapes will yield a wine that is flat, heavy, and dull. Rauner religiously has the grapes picked at about .85 acid, and allows the sugars to fall

John Rauner.

where they may. In 1980, Rauner produced a small quantity of an unusual Gewurztraminer. The grapes were harvested December 5, frozen on the vine at 18 degrees Fahrenheit. At pressing, the grapes yielded highly concentrated juice, measuring 40.4 Brix sugar. The wine was finished at 17 percent residual sugar and .88 acid.

Production in the small facility attached to the Rauner home is already over 10,000 gallons. With the anticipated construction of a new winery building, the Rauners hope to produce 50,000 gallons a year.

OTHER WASHINGTON WINERIES

Bainbridge Island Vineyard and Winery

682 State Highway 305 N.E.,
Bainbridge Island,
Washington 98110
(206) 842-WINE or 842-6711

Located a quarter mile from the Bainbridge Island ferry terminal, Joan and Gerard Bentryns' Bainbridge Island Winery is dedicated to the production of limited quantities of premium vinifera wines from western Washington grapes.

The first vines were planted in 1978. Because the Bentryns' own vineyard is quite small, a total of two acres, additional grapes are purchased from other western and south-central Washington growers. Committed to the cool climate grape varieties suited to western Washington, the Bentryns have spurred others in the Puget Sound area to grow grapes for their winery.

The Puget Sound is a very cool growing climate, and the wines are quite different from those made from grapes grown east of the Cascade Mountains. Most of the Bentryns' grape varieties are of German origin, and the wines are Germanic in style, low alcohol, crisp, off-dry to slightly sweet white wines, emphasizing delicate fruit flavors and fragrances. Muller-Thurgau is the principal variety, but Bentryn is also working with other cool climate vinifera varieties such as Madeleine Sylvaner, Madeleine Angevine, and

Siegerrebe. The wines, produced in lots as small as 25 to 80 cases, are usually available only at the winery, and sell out in a matter of days.

The winery and small wine museum are open Wednesday through Sunday, Noon to 5 PM.

Leonetti Cellar
1321 School Avenue
Walla Walla, Washington 99362
(509) 525-1428

Leonetti Cellar is Washington's easternmost winegrowing estate. Owned and operated by Gary and Nancy Figgins, Leonetti Cellar has a lengthy heritage. Figgins' grandfather, an Italian immigrant, settled in the Walla Walla Valley, growing grapes and making wines for family use. The same vineyard site, owned by Figgins' uncles, is the source of Leonetti's grapes.

The climate is similar to Washington's major winegrowing area in the south-central portion of the state, though it is more temperate year-round, and not quite as dry. Leonetti's growing site is fairly warm, averaging, according to Figgins, 2,875 heat units during the growing season.

Cabernet Sauvignon, Merlot, and Riesling are grown in the Leonetti's small vineyard. Cabernet Sauvignon, the winery's speciality, has earned this tiny winery national acclaim. The vines are severely pruned, limiting the yield to between two and three tons an acre.

Except for the yearly September release of new wines, Leonetti is not open to the public, and the wines are available only locally, and in the Seattle area.

NEUHARTH

19 Washington 81
Merlot
Aged in Oak

PRODUCED AND BOTTLED BY
NEUHARTH WINERY, INC.
SEQUIM, WA BONDED WINERY NO. WA-74
ALCOHOL 12.9% BY VOLUME

Neuharth Winery
Still Road, P.O. Box 1457
Sequim, Washington 98382
(206) 683-9652 or 683-3706

A retired grape grower from California's northern San Joaquin Valley, Eugene Neuharth and his wife Maria moved to Sequim, on Washington's Olympic Peninsula, in 1973. In 1979, the Neuharths planted thirty-three different grape varieties, mostly French-American hybrids, in two small experimental vineyards. When the Neuharths decide which varieties are best for the area, they will plant a larger vineyard.

The Olympic Peninsula is Washington's rainiest region, but Sequim's unusual microclimate is one of the driest in the western part of the state. While waiting to see how the grapes adapt to this unusual climate, Neuharth is making wines from grapes grown in the south-central portion of the state, sometimes blending these with grapes from his experimental vineyards.

Although a small winery, the Neuharths have invested in an attractive tasting room, and welcome visitors Wednesday through Sunday from Noon to 5 PM.

Quilceda Creek Vintners

5226 Machias Road
Snohomish, Washington 98290
(206) 568-2389

Quilceda Creek is a small winery specializing in one wine only—Cabernet Sauvignon. For their consulting enologist, Quilceda can claim none other than the legendary California winemaker, Andre Tchelistcheff. It so happens that Quilceda's winemaker and principal owner, Alex Golitzin, is Tchelistcheff's nephew. Golitzin, who was born in France and spent World War II in Paris, is a chemical engineering graduate from the University of California at Berkeley.

While many wineries make several different wines, it is Golitzin's philosophy to focus all his care and attention on only one variety. After several years of making small experimental batches of Cabernet Sauvignon, a corporation was formed, and the winery was bonded in 1978. Most new wineries produce a white wine of some sort that can be released the year after the winery is bonded. For Quilceda, the first release did not come until 1983. Quilceda, having no vineyards of its own, buys its Cabernet grapes from growers in south-central Washington. The winery is open to the public by appointment only.

1979
Salishan Vineyards
Washington
Pinot Noir

PRODUCED & BOTTLED BY PONZI VINEYARDS
BEAVERTON, OREGON BW-OR-56
ALCOHOL by VOLUME 12%

Salishan Vineyards
Route 2, Box 8
La Center, Washington 98629
(206) 263-2713

In 1971, Joan and Lincoln Wolverton planted 11 acres of grapes near the town of La Center in southwest Washington, thereby becoming the first winegrowers in the modern era to make a major effort with vinifera grapes in the western part of the state.

The first years were not easy. The Wolvertons had full-time jobs in Seattle, commuting to the vineyard on weekends for the back breaking pleasure of tending 9,000 vines. In the first six years, a third of the vines were lost to deer and rabbit and had to be replaced. The Wolvertons now live at the vineyard site, and Joan devotes full-time to the vineyard and winery. The climate, quite unlike Washington's major growing region in the south-central part of the state, is more similar to Oregon's northern Willamette Valley.

Although Salishan wines have been on the market since the late seventies, the winery was not bonded until 1982, the year of their first crush. Earlier Salishan wines were made at other Northwest wineries from grapes grown at Salishan's vineyard.

The pioneering effort is succeeding, and others in the La Center area are beginning to plant vineyards. Pinot Noir is proving especially good, the La Center area being one of the few growing climates in Washington suited to the grape. Salishan is open to the public most Sunday afternoons, and by appointment weekdays and Saturdays.

Vernier Wines

430-3 South 96th Street, Seattle, Washington 98108
(206) 763-3633

Named after the patron saint of Burgundy, Vernier Wines grew into being out of the home winemaking experiences of Bruce Crabtree and Mark Floren. Through Crabtree's contacts with patrons of Rosellini's Four-10 restaurant, where he is sommelier, a partnership was formed, and Vernier Wines was born. For their first crush, in 1982, Crabtree and Floren made 2,300 gallons of wine. Expansion to 10,000 gallons is expected within a few years. At the present time, Vernier is open to the public by appointment only.

Crabtree's association with fine cuisine influences his approach to winemaking. The wine that best complements food is not the fat, overwhelming, unctuous style that became so popular in America in the 70's, but a more restrained, higher acid style that cleanses the palate and unfolds to show its best throughout a meal without becoming obvious and dulling, a style epitomized by the wines of Bordeaux and Burgundy.

Chardonnay, Vernier's flagship wine, begins fermentation in a stainless steel tank at about 65 degrees, then is racked into small stainless steel barrels where the fermentation temperature drops to about 45 to 50 degrees. Sauvignon Blanc is treated in the same manner. Crabtree believes that fermenting Sauvignon Blanc for a time at a higher temperature moderates the grassy-herbaceous character that typifies most Washington renditions of the grape. Before bottling, the Sauvignon Blanc is blended with Semillon, as is done in Bordeaux. The white wines, except for the Riesling, are aged a short time in Limousin oak. Cabernet Sauvignon and Merlot, neither of which are fined or filtered, are aged much longer in the Limousin barrels.

Vernier purchases grapes from several growers, frequently blending the different batches to make the finished wines. Crabtree believes that the winemaker's art goes further than just making wine from grapes. Much of the art comes in blending the wines to achieve something better than any one of the wines would have been on its own.

Manfred Vierthaler Winery
17136 Highway 410
Sumner, Washington 98390
(206) 863-1633

Built in a Bavarian architectural style, the Manfred Vierthaler winery and restaurant is located on El-Hi Hill overlooking the Puyallup River Valley. One of the few wineries making wine from western Washington grapes, Vierthaler's vineyard is planted on the steep slope surrounding the winery, but most of the acreage is under contract with growers in the Puyallup and Carbon River Valleys near Orting. Muller-Thurgau and Riesling are the principal varieties.

In addition to the Washington grape wines, Vierthaler also makes many wines from California grape juice. The wines from the California juice have the word "American" included on the label. Some of Vierthaler's generic wine names are unique and fanciful. They include Moselle, American Rhine Rose, Late Harvest American Burgundy, and Late Harvest Rose of Pinot Noir.

Though he has lived most of his life in America, Vierthaler was born in Germany, and as described in the winery's literature, is a direct descendant of the Emperor Charlemagne, as well as some of the royal families of Bavaria. In discussing the criteria for labeling a wine "Late Harvest," Vierthaler refers to German wine laws, and speaks of sugar levels in terms of the German Oechsle scale. From Vierthaler's perspective, "Late Harvest" wines should be designated as such based solely on the sugar content of the grapes—or grape juice. From this point of view, most of the wines from California's hot Central Valley would be considered "Late Harvest"—or better.

In the same building as the winery and tasting room are two restaurants, both overlooking the Puyallup River Valley, the Roof Garden, featuring a salad and sandwich bar, and the Royal Bavarian Dining Room. Included on the menu are vineyard snails in herb butter, breaded wild boar filets, and hippopotamus roast.

Woodward Canyon Winery
Route 1, Box 387
Lowden, Washington 99360
(509) 525-2262 or 525-4129

Few wine grapes are grown in the southeastern portion of the state, but Woodward Canyon is one of the new small wineries near Walla Walla that is putting the area on the vinous map. Ray and Jean Small are Woodward Canyon's principal owners. Their son, Rick Small, is the winemaker. The winery itself does not have any vineyards, but Rick and his wife, Darcey, own a six acre Chardonnay vineyard in the hills of the Walla Walla Valley.

The Walla Walla area is relatively cooler and moister than Washington's major growing area in the south-central portion of the state. Though equipped for drip irrigation, the Smalls' six acre vineyard is usually dry-farmed.

Woodward Canyon's major effort is directed toward barrel fermented Chardonnay. Because most of the vineyard is not yet bearing, the Smalls' purchase the majority of their grapes from south-central Washington growers.

Woodward Canyon produces 3,000 gallons of wine a year. The winery is open to the public by appointment, or by chance.

IDAHO

Idaho Wineries

1. Louis Facelli Winery
2. Ste. Chapelle Vineyards
3. Weston Winery

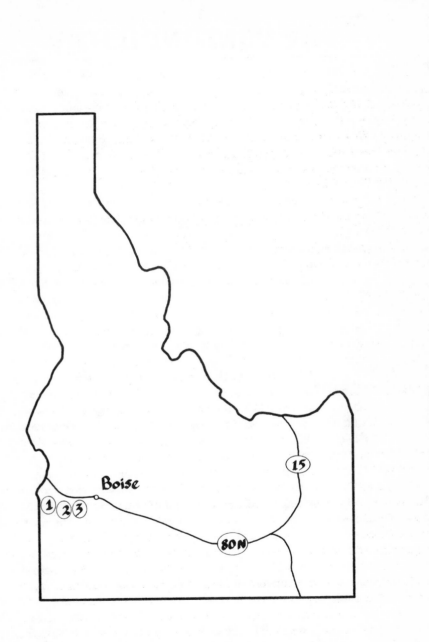

Boise

THE WINE INDUSTRY

The Idaho wine industry, the Northwest's newest, is less than a decade old. Although there were earlier pioneering attempts at winegrowing, the first vines in the modern era were not planted until the early 1970's. Ste. Chapelle Vineyards, until recently the state's only winery, did not have its first crush until 1976. Ste. Chapelle has since gone from zero production to 200,000 gallons a year, and soon, a yearly production of more than 500,000 gallons is anticipated.

Not realizing that parts of Idaho are warm and relatively temperate year-round, enophiles outside the state did not readily accept the idea that Idaho could be a viable climate for premium vinifera grape wines. Ste. Chapelle's first Riesling release established without a doubt that Idaho was indeed a viable winegrowing region. It was not too difficult to accept that Idaho could make good Riesling. After all, German Rieslings are grown in very cool growing regions, it was reasoned, and it did not seem too farfetched that Idaho might succeed with the grape. Other grape varieties, of course, would not fair nearly as well — or so went the common wisdom.

Ste. Chapelle's first Chardonnay release shattered most of the remaining misconceptions. The wine was not an austere French Chablis style of Chardonnay, but a rich, buttery, high alcohol wine not too far removed from the overblown California Chardonnays of the late 70's. Ste. Chapelle has since changed to a more elegant style to better complement food, but their first Chardonnay garnered many awards and much acclaim—and proved a point. Idaho's Snake River Valley is a flexible and excellent winegrowing climate. Gewurztraminer, Chenin Blanc, and Pinot Noir have since joined the list of Idaho wines, and other varieties, as yet in smaller quantities, have been planted to vine.

Near Lewiston, in one of the state's earliest grape growing areas, and in a few other locations, some small scale vineyard development is underway. The state's major winegrowing region, however, is centered at the western end of state in the Snake River Valley. Facelli Vineyards, the state's second winery in the modern era, began operation in 1981. Weston Winery opened the following year, and others will soon join the pace. In less than a decade, Idaho has gone from virtually nothing to what is approaching 1,000 acres of grapes.

WINEGROWING CLIMATES

Although Idaho has several areas that are suitable for winegrowing, the Snake River Valley in the southern part of the state is the only area that has yet been developed in any major way. The region's openness, its reputation as prime orchard land, and its agricultural history make the area a natural for intensive viticultural development. Most of the growing sites are clustered at the western edge of the state not far from the capital of Boise.

The broad Snake River River Valley is characterized by dry undulating terrain and small hills and valleys formed by the numerous tributaries that feed the famous Snake River. Most Northwest grape growing regions are at an elevation of less than 1,000 feet, but growing sites in Idaho's Snake River Valley, further inland, are planted at up to 3,000 feet above sea level. Warm, dry, sunny days, cool nights, and cold winters characterize the growing climate.

As might be expected, cold weather can be a problem. Frosts threaten the vines in springtime, but the greatest danger is caused by rapid wintertime temperature fluctuations. Bright sunlight reflecting off the snow cover can cause sun scalding as parts of the vines are warmed during the daytime, followed by a rapid temperature drop at nightfall. So far these dangers have been more of a threat than an actuality, and there has been little vine or crop loss.

Though a distinct growing climate, Idaho's Snake River Valley is more similar to the climate of south-central Washington than the climate of western Oregon. Grapes are typically ample in both sugar and acid. Riesling and Chardonnay are the principal grape varieties, but Pinot Noir, Chenin Blanc, Gewurztraminer, and other varieties have also been successful. Ste. Chapelle, Facelli, and Weston are all located in Idaho's Snake River Valley.

GRAPE VARIETIES

Because of the utter newness of Idaho's wine industry, an adequate assessment of grape varieties is scarcely feasible. Many vineyards in new growing sites or with grape varieties new to Idaho are not yet bearing fruit. Moreover, Idaho has few wineries, and separating a winemaker's own style from the characteristics of the region is a tenuous proposition.

At first, many viewed Idaho as a viticulturally limited region, a region that might do acceptably well with one or two varieties, but a marginal grape growing area of limited scope. Just the opposite has proven the case. Idaho is not only a quality growing region, it is a flexible one as well. As new vineyards and new varieties begin to bear fruit, new wineries come on stream, and grape growing expands to other Idaho growing areas, the depth and breadth of the the Idaho region will become more readily apparent.

CHARDONNAY put Idaho firmly on the vinous map. With the first release of Chardonnay, Idaho wine could no longer be dismissed as a vinous quirk. Those expecting Idaho Chardonnays to be, at best, austere and Chablis-like were in for a surprise. The grapes ripen well while maintaining good acidity, and the wines range in style from ripe, round, and viscous to crisp, flavorful, and elegant. Chardonnay is an excellent Idaho varietal.

CHENIN BLANC, seldom, if ever, a wine of exceptional distinction no matter where the grapes are grown, nevertheless produces very pleasant wines, usually made in a semi-dry style. In Idaho, Chenin Blanc, a late maturing variety, produces wines with a pleasant crispness that complements the grape's inherently soft character.

GEWURZTRAMINER, one of the more recent Idaho varietals, is expected to do well. The grape ripens early, withstands winter cold, and prefers relatively cool heat accumulations during the growing season. A variety from France's Alsace region, some have suggested that a sunny dry growing environment best suits the grape. By all accounts, Idaho looks like a favorable climate.

PINOT NOIR will form the foundation of Idaho's emerging sparkling wine industry. Destined, as well, to be the state's principal red wine grape, Idaho Pinot Noirs should be fairly ripe and full-bodied. As always with this fickle variety, prediction is difficult, and winegrowers may need several vintages under their belts before the grape's potential is known.

RIESLING, also called Johannisberg Riesling and White Riesling, is the grape that ushered in Idaho's wine industry. Still the industry's mainstay, Idaho Rieslings are fairly ripe and full-flavored, yet complemented by good acidity.

IDAHO WINERIES

Louis Facelli Winery
Founded 1981
P.O. Box 39, Wilder, Idaho 83676
(208) 482-7719

Daily, noon to 5 PM.

LOUIS FACELLI WINERY

Louis Facelli moved to Idaho from California in 1973. A home winemaker, Facelli found himself without ready access to vinifera wine grapes, and turned for a time to fruit and berry wines to continue his hobby.

By the latter half of the 70's, however, it was becoming apparent that Idaho's Snake River Valley was well suited to vinifera grape growing. In 1980, Facelli planted 5½ acres of vines, and envisioned a small premium winery making no more than 10,000 gallons a year—but plans change.

Facelli first made wine for commercial sale in 1981. The wines did exceptionally well in Northwest wine judgings, and Facelli had to explain, in the face of great demand, that he had made a mere 1,700 gallons of wine in a tiny twenty by thirty foot building, and he had virtually no wine to sell. At the same time, Facelli realized that a vineyard and a 10,000 gallon winery was getting too big to manage part-time, yet was too small to easily sustain itself financially. Besides running the winery, Facelli was working at as many as three other jobs. The dream of a small premium winery was succeeding, but, in part because of its success, the dream was becoming less than enjoyable.

Facelli did not give up his dream, he transformed it, joining forces with local farmers, Fred and Norm Batt, and incorporating the Louis Facelli Winery in 1982. The Batts had already planted 37 acres of grapes in 1981, east of Wilder, Idaho. In the spring of 1983, the Batts planted 120 more acres west of Wilder, in the Arena Valley. The Arena Valley vineyards face due south. The soil is more gravelly than other growing sites in the greater Snake River Valley. Since there is no underlying layer of hardpan, the vine roots penetrate the the soil easily, and special measures to rip the soil are unnecessary.

Until Facelli's vineyards mature, most of their wine will be made from Washington grapes. Facelli's rapid expansion should soon alleviate, at least in the Northwest, the scarcity of their wines. In 1982, the first year of Facelli's incorporation, production jumped to 14,000 gallons. By the mid to late 80's, Facelli will be producing 130,000 to 150,000 gallons a year. Visitors are welcome at the new winery, located in the town of Wilder, a tenth of a mile north of the Highway 95 and Highway 19 intersection.

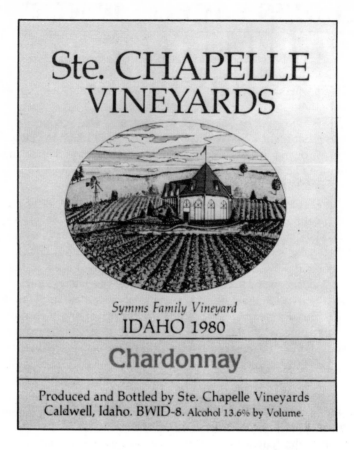

Ste. CHAPELLE VINEYARDS

Symms Family Vineyard
IDAHO 1980

Chardonnay

Produced and Bottled by Ste. Chapelle Vineyards
Caldwell, Idaho. BWID-8. Alcohol 13.6% by Volume.

Ste. Chapelle Vineyards
Founded 1976
Route 4, Box 775, Caldwell, Idaho 83605
(208) 459-7222

Monday through Saturday, Noon to 5 PM.

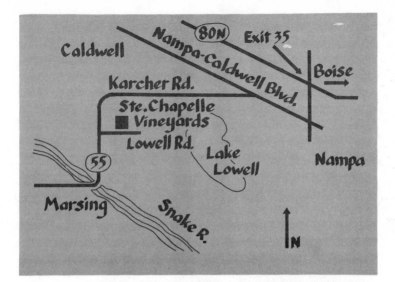

STE. CHAPELLE
VINEYARDS

Ste. Chapelle Vineyards is a remarkable success story, beginning its existence as the first winery in a virtually untested new winegrowing region, and developing almost instantly into one of the most important forces in the Northwest wine industry.

Ste. Chapelle will soon reach a production of more than a half million gallons a year, and the wines, available in most of the 50 states, have garnered an enviable track record in regional, national, and international wine judgings—all this from a winery and wine industry that was literally non-existent a decade ago. New Idaho wineries have since started operation, but to most people, Ste. Chapelle is still virtually synonymous with Idaho wine. Because of Ste. Chapelle, Idaho has come further, faster than any other Northwest winegrowing state.

The winery is a corporation owned by Bill Broich, Ste. Chapelle's winemaker, and the Symms family, long-time Idaho fruit growers. Vines were planted in the early 1970's, and in 1976, Ste. Chapelle had its first commercial crush.

The winery is styled after a Paris chapel.

Ste. Chapelle began its existence in, what must have seemed to most, a financial and meteorological climate of great uncertainty. Many outside the state have the conception that potatoes and snow are Idaho's only viable crops, yet the Snake River Valley has long been noted for its orchards of cherries, pears, apples, peaches, and other fruits. It has been said that any area that can successfully grow peaches is also suitable for vinifera wine grapes. The overwhelming success of Ste. Chapelle's vineyards and wines does not contradict this maxim. At an elevation of 2,500 feet, the area is the highest major growing region in the Northwest.

Ste. Chapelle's winegrowing climate is more similar to that of south-central Washington than the climate of Oregon's major grape growing areas. Warm, dry, sunny days, cool nights, and cold winters characterize the climate. In cooler Oregon, vines are cane pruned, but like Washington, Idaho vines can be cordon pruned, a less troublesome and time consuming method that prunes and trains two permanent canes into lateral arms called cordons. From these cordons sprout each seasons new growth. After the harvest, the seasonal canes are pruned away, leaving the lateral cordons and the vine trunk to form a stylized "T." Grape yields have been good with this method, six tons an acre for Chardonnay and Riesling.

As might be expected, cold weather can be a problem. Frosts are a springtime threat. Winter cold is also potentially damaging, but the vines are endangered most by rapid temperature fluctuations caused by Idaho's sunny winter days. Bright sunlight reflecting off the snow cover can cause sun scalding as parts of the vines are warmed to fifty or sixty degrees during the daytime, followed by a rapid temperature drop to zero degrees at nightfall. In spite of the adversity, there has been little vine loss.

There are, however, other threats. Wine industries in other states worry about convincing legislatures to pass laws giving additional support to the winegrowing industry. In Idaho, wineries worry about convincing their state legislature not to pass laws that would destroy the industry. Idaho, particularly the southern portion of the state where the winegrowing industry is centered, is heavily influenced by a large anti-alcohol/anti-wine populace, and the pioneering efforts of the fledgling wine industry are not always appreciated. The Idaho wine industry faces a continuing battle to stay alive and well. In one legislative session, for example, an outdoor advertising bill was introduced that would have made it illegal for Idaho wineries to display their name on their own mailbox.

Like many Oregon wineries, Ste. Chapelle made some of their first wines from Washington grapes while waiting for their own state's vines to mature. Oregon is gradually phasing out the use of Washington grapes, but Ste. Chapelle, in part because of the lack of support and the legislative threat within the state, is looking to Washington for additional vineyard acreage as well as a second winery.

Expansion within Idaho continues as well. Ste. Chapelle will soon be the Northwest's largest producer of sparkling wines. The initial 2,000 gallon a year production will be expanding to an estimated 30,000 gallons a year with completion of a new facility devoted solely to sparkling wine production. The cuvee is 100 percent Idaho Pinot Noir. Eighty more acres of the grape were planted in 1982, not only for the sparkling wine, but also for a red still wine.

Not unexpectedly, Riesling was Ste. Chapelle's first wine from Idaho grapes, soon followed by Chardonnay, Chenin Blanc, Gewurztraminer, and Pinot Noir. Many could accept the idea that Idaho was capable of producing Riesling, a cool climate grape that

The tasting room.

shows well even when underripe, but when Ste. Chapelle released a successful Chardonnay, it was a revelation, a confirmation
that Idaho was not merely a winegrowing curiosity, but a broadly
based winegrowing climate, a stellar new wine region.

Getting the grapes to ripen has not been a problem. Ste.
Chapelle's 1978 and 1979 Chardonnays have been the most consistently successful wines in Northwest competitions and have
received considerable national acclaim. The wines were made in
the overripe, high alcohol, low acid style that until recently typified
the American conception of premium Chardonnay. These wines,
highly successful in their own way, demonstrated that Idaho has
no difficulty ripening grapes.

In 1980, pleased with the success of the wines, but not fully
satisfied with the wines themselves, Broich made a conscious decision to alter the style of their Chardonnay, taking advantage of
Idaho's ability to maintain adequate acid, and ripen grapes at lower
sugar levels. The result was a better balanced, more elegant wine,
a wine more attuned to harmonizing with food. The wine was
entered in Britain's International Wine and Spirits Competition,
receiving a gold medal, and garnering the highest score of any of
the 960 American wines in the competition.

Ste. Chapelle's winery is distinctive and striking. Designed
by architect Nat Adams from photographs of the Ste. Chapelle

250

chapel in Paris, its octagonal roof reaches a peak 52 feet above the winery floor. Multiple windows, 24 feet high, allow a panoramic view of the vineyards and the broad, gently sloping valley below. The tasting room and reception area are finished in oak, and contribute to the winery's warm atmosphere. By right and example, Ste. Chapelle is the showcase for Idaho's new wine industry.

"THE RIVER RUNNER"
1982
IDAHO
WHITE RIESLING

PRODUCED AND BOTTLED BY WESTON WINERY
SUNNYSLOPE, CALDWELL, IDAHO   BWID 13
Alcohol 10.5% by Volume
Residual Sugar 4.42% by Weight

Weston Winery
Founded 1982
Route 4, Box 759, Caldwell, Idaho 83605
(208) 454-1682
May through October, daily, Noon to 6 PM. November through April, Wednesday through Sunday, Noon to 6 PM.
